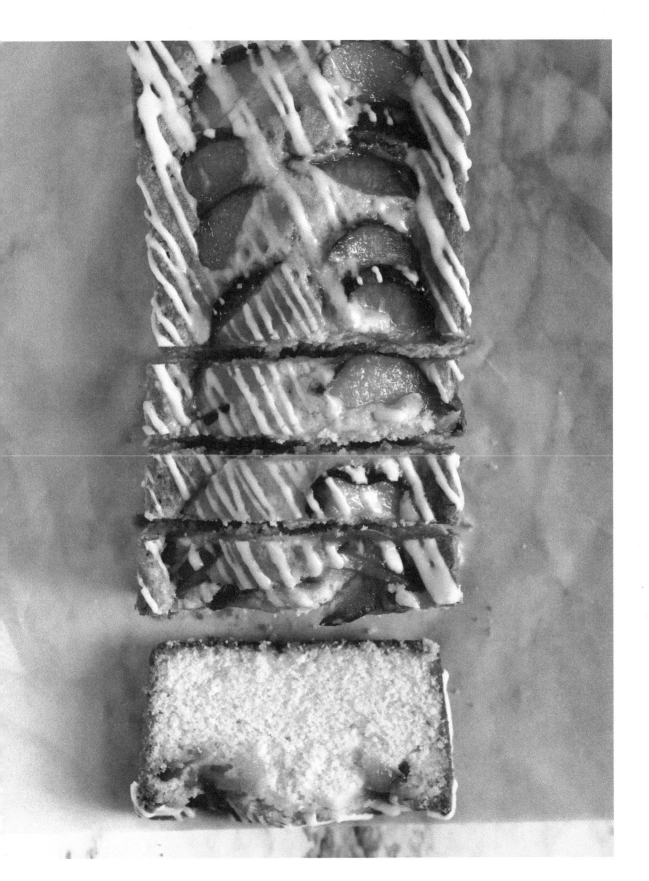

SUGAR HIGH

SWEET & SAVORY BAKING IN YOUR HIGH-ALTITUDE KITCHEN

NICOLE HAMPTON

OF THE BLOG

WESTWINDS
PRESS®

CONTENTS

BAKING THROUGH DOUGH EYES

Baking has always been a part of my life. I started baking with my mom at a really young age, before I could even reach the counter. We baked cookies from scratch, and sometimes pulled out my grandma's recipe for peanut brittle, but otherwise we used a lot of boxed mixes. (I'll admit, to this day, sometimes I just crave a good ol' reliable box-mix cake.)

As I grew up, I started to experiment more with from-scratch baking, and you probably know how that went. I've lived at a high altitude for most of my life, and I've had a shocking number of failures in the kitchen.

When I first started blogging, I lived down near sea level in Boston, but I had an apartment-sized oven, which was a whole new struggle. When I moved in, I didn't even know that apartment-sized ovens were a thing. After finally building a collection of bakeware that actually fit in my oven, it was about time to move back home to the original struggle of baking at high altitude.

Cupcakes were my first stop. Listen, there are few things more disappointing than driving to the grocery store, buying all the stuff, and spending huge amounts of time measuring and mixing just to pull sunken, dense, eggy messes from the oven. For the longest time, I couldn't get the flavors right and I couldn't get the texture right. Even after all my experimenting, I still think that homemade cakes are one of the hardest things to make at altitude.

As hard as normal cakes are, for some reason chocolate cakes are in a whole other league. Chocolate cake batter always looks so luscious and silky, and I would think, "Yes, this is the one. It's gonna be perfect." Then I'd pull it out of the oven thirty minutes later to find that the middle had collapsed nearly all the way to the bottom of the cake pan, and that the rest was full of giant, gaping air pockets.

It's just a bummer that baking at altitude requires so much trial and error. You put something in the oven, tasting great and looking right, and then your oven (and mine too) pulls some kind of mean magic trick in there. The good news is that baking is a science, and high-altitude baking has solutions. I'm here to show them to you.

Don't get me wrong—I still burn Pop-Tarts® in the toaster oven at work, and I still have to fan smoke out of my kitchen with a dishtowel on occasion. But I do have some really reliable recipes that have had my back when I need to make a cake in a rush, or when I need to whip up a pie for a last-minute party.

Nowadays, it makes me feel more confident in the kitchen knowing that I can pull out my recipe box and choose any cake, bread, pie, or bar and it'll work. No mean tricks from the oven! Baking is way more fun when it actually turns out beautifully in the end.

I hope that, through this book, you can find enjoyment in baking again, and that you, too, can have a secret stash of recipes that just do their thing in the oven and make you look good! Having a kitchen full of yummy treats ain't so bad either.

HIGH-ALTITUDE BAKING TIPS

As someone who grew up in a high-altitude area, I always thought baking was harder than it really is. I constantly wondered how people were ever making homemade cakes work. I always heard people saying that baking is a science, and, of course, that's true. But no matter how strictly I measured or how carefully I let my eggs come to room temperature, good things were just not happening.

Why are things so painfully different at high altitude? And how can you fix it? This book will give you the answers and show you how to bake things you actually want to eat on a regular basis. (I will refuse all responsibility for any weight gain due to the improvement of your baking skills.)

WHAT YOU MIGHT BE EXPERIENCING

While different types of baked goods have a different set of difficulties at altitude, there are some common things you might be seeing:

- Cakes or cupcakes that look perfect while baking, but immediately sink in the center after they come out of the oven.
- Overly airy cakes and cupcakes that have large holes throughout.
- Cakes that are extremely dense, and taste and smell very eggy.
- Dense batters that take forever to bake through, resulting in an overcooked exterior and a raw center.
- Baked goods that have less flavor than you expect, even though you add salt, and vanilla, and other should-be-delicious things to flippin' everything.

- Yeast breads that seem to fail for, like, every single reason.
- Making all of these problems worse, your normal baking solutions and fix-its don't seem to have the desired effect on your baking.

You guys, I have been there. But we're gonna fix it together.

COMMON MYTHS ABOUT HIGH-ALTITUDE BAKING

Honestly, I always felt like the resources for this were so limited. For a really long time, my best guess as to what to do was to add more flour to literally everything. Turns out, that's not how it works. Let's start with some misconceptions about baking at a high altitude:

- Adding flour solves everything: Adding flour is my go-to fix for cake issues, and it certainly does help with certain recipes. However, liquid actually evaporates more quickly at higher altitudes, which means that, in some cases, all adding flour will do is simply dry out your dish. Depending on what you're baking, additional eggs, reduced sugar, or reduced leavening could be your solution, not extra flour.
- Cookies are affected as much as anything else: This is not an all-encompassing statement, but for the most part, cookies are less affected by altitude than other baked goods. I try most cookie recipes without any modifications first, or I might reduce the leavening as a first step. If you reduce leavening in any recipe, start with reducing it by ⅛ teaspoon for every 1 teaspoon of the leavening agent called for.

- More baking powder/soda fixes sinking cakes: In fact, the reason that cakes sink at higher altitudes is because the leavening agent rises much faster up here, causing the cake to rise much too quickly. Then, it proceeds to fall and ruin your day. Reducing your baking powder or baking soda slightly, rather than increasing it, can help prevent cakes from sinking.
- Adding more salt will help with the lack of flavor: Of course, you should add at least a pinch of salt to any baked item, but at a high altitude, lack of salt is likely not the issue. Since liquids evaporate faster up here during baking, you'll actually want to add more liquid to your recipe if flavor is an issue. Too much liquid may change the entire texture of the dough or batter, but usually a couple of teaspoons extra of oil, milk, or other liquid helps with flavor.
- Letting yeast dough rise longer helps: Yeast breads are the bane of my existence. They're definitely the most challenging types of high-altitude recipes for me. Again, the leavening is going to rise much faster here, so you'll actually want to let the dough rise for less time than normal. It's also common for folks to use cold water instead of warm, or to punch down the dough more frequently to help slow down the rise.

HIGH ALTITUDE AND YOUR RECIPES

Now that we have these basics out of the way, let's get down to the recipes. Let's talk through how several types of recipes are affected by altitude, and what you can do to make them work. You don't have to experiment blindly; if you have the right tips and tricks in place, you can really make most recipes work. The next time you see a pretty cake on Pinterest, or some adorable dinner rolls shaped like bunnies, these tips will help

you give them a shot with confidence.

Before trying a new recipe, read through these tips and tricks to help make it successful the first time around. Keep in mind that the same things that work for cake recipes won't do the trick for bread, and vice versa. Get settled in, I got you.

Quick breads, scones, and muffins: These types of baked goods that aren't super sweet, and also aren't made using yeast, are usually fairly simple to make, but you should still keep some adaption tips in mind:

- Of all types of baking recipes, quick breads are most important to avoid overmixing. Most of the time, unless indicated otherwise, you want the end batter or dough to still be lumpy.
- It's important to achieve a golden-brown top for these baked goods. If you aren't reaching it at the suggested oven temperature, increase it by 25°F, and decrease the baking time.
- Moisture can be an issue at altitude, particularly with muffins. Consider adding another 2 to 3 teaspoons of whatever liquid you are using in the batter, or of water. Another option is to add ¼ cup of sour cream to a muffin recipe that yields 12 muffins.

Yeast breads: The first time that you make a perfect loaf of bread, or the perfect cinnamon rolls, it's a truly joyous occasion. I'm talkin' Champagne all around. Here are some tips and tricks for bread recipes:

- Decrease your total rising time when working with yeast bread; you can even put the dough in the refrigerator to slow down the rising process.
- Pay close attention to the actual size of the dough (you'll see cues in the recipes, for example, "…until doubled in size") more than the rise time. Rising often happens

more quickly at altitude, so you want to watch it closely to ensure that the dough isn't overproofed.

- Decrease your goal size for the dough. When a recipe calls for the dough to double in size, move on to the next step just before it has doubled. This helps avoid overproofing as well.
- Place a small pan half full of water on the bottom shelf of the oven while baking. This isn't always needed, but it can help develop a sturdy crust on loaves of bread.
- Baking temperatures don't usually need to be changed for bread, but on occasion the crust can form too early if the baking temperature is too high. If this happens, cover the bread with foil for the remaining baking time.

Cakes: If you've got a cake recipe that isn't working for you, here are some things you can try to adjust:

- Decrease the leavening agent in the recipe by ⅛ to ¼ teaspoon, depending on how much the recipe calls for. If it calls for less than a teaspoon, go for a ⅛ teaspoon reduction. If it's more than a teaspoon, go for a ¼ teaspoon reduction.
- Increase the baking temperature by 25°F, and bake it for a shorter amount of time— this is particularly helpful for cakes that are sinking.
- Add ¼ to ½ cup extra flour to the recipe.
- Take care not to overmix cake batters, especially when working with eggs. Over-beaten eggs can create those pesky large air pockets and contribute to too-fast rising.
- Grease your cake pans very well! Rumor has it that cake batters sticks more in high altitude. I prepare most of my cake pans with this mix: equal parts room-temperature shortening, canola oil, and flour. Beat the ingredients together until

completely smooth, and store the mixture in the fridge. When a recipe calls for greasing a pan, I spread a thin layer in the baking pan with a brush or paper towel before pouring in my batter or dough. If a recipe calls for greasing and flouring the pan, I add extra flour to the pan after greasing with this mixture, rotate the pan to coat it evenly, and then shake out the excess.

To unmold cake layers from pans, I always let the cake cool at least slightly in the pan. I run a clean butter knife around all the edges, and the cake should then tip right out. If you have issues with the cake sticking on the bottom, gently pry the cake around the edges with the knife to loosen.

Cookies: As I mentioned before, cookies are generally the least affected item when it comes to high-altitude adaptations. However, there are still some modifications to remember if you're working with a cookie that isn't turning out quite right:

- It can be tough to find the right baking time for cookies. Most recipes give a range for baking times, mainly because you have to keep an eye on the cookies in those last few minutes to avoid under or overbaking. I suggest doing a test batch with only one or two cookies, which will help you figure out the right baking time in the oven.
- Many people worry about overmixing, and of course it's important to avoid. But at your last stage of mixing, whenever the last set of ingredients go in, make sure you get everything completely and properly incorporated, even if it seems like you are mixing for a long time. Otherwise, you'll end up with an uneven batch of cookies that don't turn out uniformly.
- I do still occasionally reduce the leavening agent in cookies to avoid a too-puffy cookie. Use the same tips as for cake here.

Bars: Bars can be a bit complex, even without the challenges of baking them at altitude. But adjusting for the right results is important.

- Getting the right balance between too wet and too dry for any bar recipe is important. If you try a recipe, and it's too wet or won't set in the oven, consider adding ¼ cup flour and reducing the baking temperature. Remember to also increase the overall baking time.
- On the other hand, if a recipe is ending up dry and brittle, add 1 to 2 tablespoons of butter or oil, or another egg, to the recipe.
- Once again, you'll need to pay close attention to the baking time in order to achieve a fully cooked center and to avoid overcooked edges.

GETTING IT RIGHT

I'd like to end this section with a few words of encouragement. Living near the mountains is fun for a million reasons, but baking just isn't always one of them. What got me to a confident place in the kitchen, while living way up here at over five thousand feet above sea level, was finding a few basic recipes that worked, and sticking with them. (And, also, a few drinks here and there in the kitchen. It's cool—sometimes I bake with alcohol, sometimes I just bake near it.) Seriously though, I hope this book gives you not just a few great basic recipes, but also a kitchen that smells of cinnamon, and brown sugar, and bread, and chocolate, pretty much all the time.

Happy baking—you got this!

TOOLS

Let's talk about some more of the nitty-gritty: which tools are essential, and which are just helpful to have around.

First, what you need:
- Bakeware of many kinds. You'll want baking sheets, muffin pans, and cake pans, in a variety of shapes—round, square, rectangle, and loaf. It's also a good idea to have a springform pan and at least one Bundt pan.
- Box grater or shredder with both wide and thin shredding widths. Alternatively, you can use a wide shredder and a zester.
- Cake testers to test the doneness of cakes. You can buy an actual cake tester tool, or just use a toothpick or thin skewer. I find that any of these options provides what you need!
- Double boiler for slowly cooking egg whites and sugar for buttercreams, and gently heating chocolate. You could also use a heatproof bowl set over a pot of hot water; just make sure the bowl isn't touching the water in the pot.
- Electric hand mixer, even if it's just a super cheap one you found at a garage sale. Honestly, it's so hard to achieve the right textures without it, plus who wants to spend thirty minutes whipping cream by hand?
- Instant-read thermometer to measure the temperature of water and milk before adding yeast, and to make sure everything is just right. Working with yeast can be tricky, and thermometers take the guesswork out.
- Measuring spoons and cups to make sure everything is properly measured, of course! Dry measuring cups for dry ingredients and liquid measuring cups—the glass ones with a spout—for liquids. Trust me, guys—it makes a difference!
- Mixing bowls in several sizes, at least some of them microwave- and heat-safe. You'll use these to mix batters and doughs.
- Offset spatula to spread and frost. Simply put, this is the kitchen tool that you never knew you needed. I use the small 5- or 6-inch ones the most, even on big cakes.
- Parchment paper or nonstick baking mats to keep things from sticking, and to limit the number of times you have to wash those big pans.
- Pastry blender for when you don't have a food processor, or maybe just don't feel like pulling it out or cleaning it. You'll use this tool to make pie crusts and biscuits and scones—any recipe that involves cutting butter or shortening into flour.
- Pastry brush for applying flavorings to cake layers before filling and frosting.
- Rolling pin to roll out all those pretty pie crusts or cookie doughs just right. I have a whole collection, but my favorite is just a plain old, simple wood one. Go with whatever kind you are comfortable with!
- Rubber spatulas to scrape out all the good stuff from the mixing bowls when you're ready to bake.
- Whisks to stir ingredients, both dry and wet alike, and to marry them together in the end.

Now, what's nice to have:
- Biscuit cutters or just a mason jar lid—that'll work too. Or a knife and a steady hand. Or an old cookie cutter. I'm flexible.
- Food processor to help you easily make that pie crust and crush graham crackers for crusts and toppings.
- Piping bags and tips to make cupcakes pretty, and to make frosting cakes much more easy. Spatulas will work too, though!
- Stand mixer to help you multitask in the kitchen, and to do all the hard work for you along the way.

INGREDIENTS

It's not always easy to get great ingredients—maybe your grocery store just isn't equipped for it, or it's more money than you'd like to spend. Whatever the reason, I understand. And it's not always necessary. As I write this, we're going through a vanilla shortage, making it insanely expensive, so I constantly hunt for deals or just opt for imitation. It's fine, really.

One of the areas where you can't skip the right ingredient, however, is with **flour**. Most of the recipes could be made with all-purpose flour, but when a recipe calls for cake flour or bread flour, it really does matter. I've done my best to keep these to only the completely necessary ingredients in this book. If you can't find cake flour, you can take a 1 cup measure, scoop 2 tablespoons of cornstarch into the bottom, and fill the rest with all-purpose flour. Whisk, and you've got 1 cup of cake flour. Self-rising flour is also something you can create at home—simply measure 1½ teaspoons of baking powder into the bottom of a 1-cup measure, and fill the rest with all-purpose flour. Whisk, and that makes 1 cup of self-rising flour!

I use several types of **sugar** throughout these recipes. Granulated white sugar is your basic sugar blended into batters and doughs alike, and it should be the easiest to find at any grocery store. For brown sugar, I usually prefer dark brown sugar, as it's got a nice flavor punch. However, I've never had an issue swapping out dark and light in recipes, so use what you have! Powdered sugar, a.k.a. confectioners' sugar, is something I often use in frostings, but it's also great in shortbread cookies and pie crusts to achieve just the right texture. Last, there's coarse sugar, which I use to top baked goods like muffins and loaf cakes. I find mine in the sprinkles section of the grocery store or online. You can also use organic raw sugar, sometimes called turbinado sugar, for this purpose.

When I'm baking with **chocolate**, I'm not picky. I usually use whatever chocolate I prefer to eat, including chocolate chips. To melt any type or amount of chocolate, I start by first chopping it into small, even pieces, then reserving about one-fourth of the chocolate. I put the rest in a clean, dry, microwave-safe bowl and microwave it full power for 30 seconds. Then, I stir the chocolate and return it to the microwave in 30-second intervals, stirring in between, until it's completely melted. I then immediately stir in the reserved chocolate until it is also melted, and I'm good to go! (Reserving some of the chocolate to stir in afterwards helps prevent an overheated result, and it keeps things smooth.)

Another item to note is **cocoa powder**. I simply cannot get that deep chocolate flavor from plain cocoa powder, so I always, always use dark cocoa powder. It's worth it, and at least in my neck of the woods, it's the same price as the regular stuff anyways.

Let's talk about **salt**. There are so many different kinds of salt out there, but for simplicity, I have always used simple table salt in baking. I think the finer grain melds and mixes just right into batters and doughs, and I always have it on hand.

Last, all the **eggs** I ever use in life are large. Substituting with medium or extra-large will have a big effect, especially at altitude, and large are the ones that are most widely available. When it comes to separating your eggs, I usually just use the shells, tossing the yolk from shell to shell to separate the parts. Another method that might be easier for you would be to use your hands, letting the white slip between your fingers into a separate bowl. Whichever you choose, just remember that whites can't have even a trace of yolk in order to behave the way it should!

Otherwise, guys, just use what you feel comfortable with, what's available to you, and it'll work!

BISCUITS, SCONES, MUFFINS & QUICK BREADS

CLASSIC BISCUITS

These biscuits are everything. Make them as a side for dinner, make them to pair with gravy, and make them just to munch on. Biscuits are so much easier to make than I thought they were, and they are so worth every minute of effort!

MAKES ABOUT 16 BISCUITS

4 cups all-purpose flour

2 tablespoons sugar

2 tablespoons baking powder

2 teaspoons salt

1 cup shortening, chilled and cubed

1½ cups chilled buttermilk

4 tablespoons unsalted butter, melted

Line 2 baking sheets with parchment paper or nonstick baking mats. In a large bowl, stir together the flour, sugar, baking powder, and salt. Using a pastry cutter or your fingertips, cut in the shortening until the mixture has small, pea-sized chunks of shortening throughout. Stir in the buttermilk until a dough begins to form.

Turn the dough out onto a floured work surface and knead gently until the dough comes together completely, being careful not to overwork it. Using a rolling pin, roll the dough into a long rectangle, and then fold it into thirds. Roll it out into a rectangle again, about ¾ inch thick. Using a 2-inch round cutter, cut out as many rounds as you can. You can re-knead, fold, and cut the dough scraps once, but any more than that will compromise the texture of your biscuits. Place the biscuits onto your baking sheets, spacing them evenly.

Chill the biscuits in the refrigerator for 20 minutes. Don't skip this step! Try as we might, most people (myself included) overwork biscuit dough. A rest period in the refrigerator helps everything go back to the right temperature for baking. While the dough is chilling, preheat the oven to 400°F.

Brush the tops of the biscuits generously with the melted butter, and bake until risen and just golden on top, 13 to 15 minutes. Enjoy warm or at room temperature.

CHEDDAR, BACON & HERB BISCUITS

These bacon-, cheese-, and herb-flecked biscuits are hearty and savory, and they make a great breakfast. You can use whatever kind of hard, shreddable cheese that you prefer, but cheddar really shines in this recipe.

Preheat the oven to 400°F and line a baking sheet with parchment paper or a nonstick mat. In a large bowl, mix together the flour, sugar, baking powder, salt, pepper, and herbs. With a pastry blender or your fingertips, cut in the shortening until the mixture has small, pea-sized chunks of shortening throughout. Stir in the cheese and bacon. Stir in the buttermilk until just combined.

Turn out the dough onto a floured work surface. Pat the dough into a square about ½ inch thick. Using a large knife, cut the dough into 10 to 12 square biscuits, and place onto your baking sheet. Brush the tops with milk and sprinkle coarse sea salt over the top. Bake until the biscuits are golden brown on top, 13 to 15 minutes. Enjoy warm or at room temperature.

MAKES 10 TO 12 BISCUITS

2 cups all-purpose flour

1 tablespoon sugar

3 teaspoons baking powder

1 teaspoon salt

½ teaspoon freshly ground black pepper

2 teaspoons chopped fresh herbs of your choice

½ cup shortening, chilled and cubed

1 cup shredded cheddar cheese

2 to 3 tablespoons crumbled cooked bacon

¾ cup buttermilk

Milk

Coarse sea salt

ROASTED GARLIC & CARAMELIZED ONION BISCUITS

If you read my blog, you may have noticed that I'm kind of into caramelized onions. And roasted garlic is the little sister to caramelized onions. Throw them together in a biscuit, and you've got something beautiful.

MAKES 16 BISCUITS

FOR THE ROASTED GARLIC

1 large head garlic

½ teaspoon olive oil

FOR THE CARAMELIZED ONIONS

¾ cup diced onion

1 tablespoon olive oil

1 teaspoon sugar

¼ teaspoon salt

¼ teaspoon freshly ground
   black pepper

FOR THE BISCUITS

4 cups all-purpose flour

2 tablespoons sugar

2 tablespoons baking powder

1 teaspoon salt

1 teaspoon dried oregano

½ teaspoon freshly ground
   black pepper

½ teaspoon garlic powder

½ teaspoon onion powder

¾ cup shortening, chilled and cubed

1½ cups chilled buttermilk

4 tablespoons unsalted butter,
   melted

For the roasted garlic: Preheat the oven to 400°F. Cut off the top of the head of garlic to expose most of the tops of the cloves in the head. Place the garlic, cut-side up, in a square of foil, and begin to wrap the foil around the head of garlic, leaving the top open. Drizzle the olive oil over the top of the garlic. Close the foil around the top completely. Place in the oven, and bake until the garlic is golden and soft when you stick a fork into it, 45 to 60 minutes. Let cool completely. Working over a cutting board, turn the head of garlic upside down, and squeeze the cloves out of it, turning while you do so to get all of the cloves out. Use a fork to pick out any that don't fall out on their own. Smash the garlic cloves into a paste using the fork—it doesn't have to be perfectly smooth. Transfer to a bowl and refrigerate.

For the caramelized onions: In a small skillet over medium-high heat, stir together the diced onion, olive oil, and sugar. Cook, stirring occasionally, until the onion has caramelized on all sides and has cooked down to about ¼ cup, 15 to 20 minutes. Sprinkle in the salt and pepper, and place in the refrigerator to chill for at least 15 minutes.

For the biscuits: Line 2 baking sheets with parchment paper or nonstick mats. In a large bowl, stir together the flour, sugar, baking powder, salt, oregano, pepper, garlic powder, and onion powder. Using a pastry cutter or your fingertips, cut in the shortening and the reserved roasted garlic and onions until the

mixture has small, pea-sized chunks of shortening throughout. Stir in the buttermilk until a dough begins to form. Turn the dough out onto a floured work surface and knead gently until the dough comes together completely, being careful not to overwork it.

Using a rolling pin, roll the dough into a long rectangle, and then fold it into thirds. Roll it out into a rectangle again, about ¾ inch thick, straightening the edges. Using a large knife, cut into 16 even pieces. Place the dough onto the baking sheets, spacing them evenly. Chill the biscuits in the refrigerator for 20 minutes to rest the dough. While the dough is chilling, preheat the oven to 400°F.

Brush the tops of the biscuits generously with the melted butter and bake until risen and just golden on top, 13 to 15 minutes. Enjoy warm.

CANDIED WALNUT–DARK CHOCOLATE BISCUITS

These biscuits take things to another level. They use not just walnuts, but candied walnuts. And they don't use just chocolate, but dark chocolate. Seriously, these babies are fantastic.

For the candied walnuts: Preheat the oven to 250°F and line a baking sheet with foil. In a bowl, mix together the walnuts, brown sugar, honey, cinnamon, and salt. Spread evenly on the pan. Bake for 30 minutes, stirring every 10 minutes. They will look wet and the mixture will be easy to move around. Remove immediately from the pan and let the nuts cool on a sheet of parchment or a cutting board—the mixture will harden as it cools. When cool, roughly chop.

For the biscuits: Preheat the oven to 400°F and line a baking sheet with parchment paper or a nonstick mat. In a food processor, pulse together the flour, baking powder, and salt. Add the shortening and pulse just a couple of times, until the shortening is cut into pea-sized pieces. Add the buttermilk, and pulse until a dough begins to form. Place the dough on a floured work surface and knead in the chopped walnuts and the chocolate chunks. Pat the dough until it's about ¾ inch thick. Using a biscuit cutter, cut out as many biscuits as you can, then pat together the scraps to get a few more biscuits. Place the biscuits on your baking sheet, spacing them evenly. Brush the tops of the biscuits with the cream. Bake until the tops are golden, 12 to 15 minutes. Serve warm to get that melty chocolate moment!

MAKES ABOUT 8 BISCUITS

FOR THE CANDIED WALNUTS

½ cup walnuts

2 tablespoons firmly packed brown sugar

2 teaspoons honey

½ teaspoon ground cinnamon

Pinch of salt

FOR THE BISCUITS

2 cups all-purpose flour

3 teaspoons baking powder

Pinch of salt

½ cup shortening, chilled and cubed

¾ cup buttermilk

⅓ cup dark chocolate chunks or chips

1 tablespoon heavy cream

SAVORY SCONES

I can't remember who introduced me to savory scones, but that person is
a true hero. These ones are full of caramelized onions, cheddar cheese,
and crumbled sausage. They're basically a full breakfast in scone form.

MAKES 8 TO 10 SCONES

1 tablespoon unsalted butter, plus
6 tablespoons, chilled and cubed

1 large yellow onion, diced

5 tablespoons sugar

2 teaspoons salt

1½ teaspoon freshly ground
black pepper

2½ cups all-purpose flour

1 tablespoon baking powder

1 teaspoon garlic powder

1 teaspoon Italian seasoning mix

½ pound bulk pork breakfast
sausage, cooked, crumbled,
and drained

¾ cup shredded cheddar cheese

½ cup plus 1 tablespoon
heavy cream

1 tablespoon sour cream

1 egg

In a skillet over medium heat, melt 1 tablespoon of the
butter. Add the diced onion, 1 tablespoon of the sugar,
½ teaspoon salt, and ½ teaspoon pepper. Stir and cook
until the onions have reached a dark caramel color,
about 10 minutes. Set aside to cool.

In a large bowl, stir together the flour, the remaining
4 tablespoons sugar, the baking powder, the remaining
1½ teaspoon salt and 1 teaspoon pepper, the garlic
powder, and Italian seasoning. Using a pastry blender,
cut the 6 tablespoons cubed butter into the flour
mixture until the mixture resembles coarse meal,
with butter pieces the size of peas. Stir in the cooked
sausage, cheese, and caramelized onions.

In another bowl, whisk together ½ cup of the cream
with the sour cream and the egg. Pour the cream
mixture into the flour mixture, and stir until a dough
starts to form. Cover and refrigerate the mixture for
about 30 minutes.

Preheat the oven to 425°F and line a baking sheet with
parchment paper or a nonstick mat. Remove the dough
from the refrigerator and turn it out onto a floured
work surface. Use your hands to press the dough
together into a cohesive round. Form the dough into a
long rectangle about 1 inch thick. Using a large knife,
cut the dough into triangles and transfer them to
the baking sheet. Brush the tops with the remaining
1 tablespoon cream. Bake until the tops are golden
brown, 12 to 15 minutes. Cool before serving.

ORANGE CREAM SCONES

Scones always make me feel like I should be drinking tea
out of a fancy teacup, and why not? The delicate orange flavor
of these scones is boosted by the sweet orange glaze on top.

For the scones: Preheat the oven to 425°F and line
2 baking sheets with parchment paper or nonstick
mats. In a large bowl, whisk together the flour,
granulated sugar, orange zest, baking powder,
baking soda, and salt. Use a pastry blender or your
fingertips to cut in the cold butter until the mixture
resembles coarse meal. There should still be chunks
of butter throughout about the size of peas.

In another bowl, mix together the buttermilk, sour
cream, and egg. Then pour the buttermilk mixture
into the flour mixture. Use a spatula to mix until the
dough mostly holds together. Turn the dough onto a
lightly floured work surface and pat the dough into
a disk about ½ inch thick. Use a 2-inch cutter or a
large knife to make round or square scones, and
place on your baking sheets, spacing them evenly.
Brush the cream over the tops. Bake until just golden
brown, 10 to 12 minutes. Let cool.

For the glaze: In a bowl, mix together the powdered
sugar, cream, and orange zest with a fork. Dip the
cooled scones in the glaze, and let it set completely
before serving, about 20 minutes.

MAKES ABOUT 8 SCONES

FOR THE SCONES

2 cups plus 3 tablespoons
all-purpose flour

⅓ cup granulated sugar

2 tablespoons finely grated
orange zest

1 tablespoon baking powder

⅛ teaspoon baking soda

1 teaspoon salt

6 tablespoons unsalted butter,
chilled and cubed

½ cup plus 2 tablespoons chilled
buttermilk

1 tablespoon sour cream

1 egg

1 to 2 tablespoons heavy cream

FOR THE GLAZE

1 cup powdered sugar

3 to 4 tablespoons heavy cream

1 tablespoon finely grated
orange zest

BLUEBERRY MUFFINS

Blueberries, in my opinion, are best when folded into the sweet, light batter of a muffin. These are everything you want in a blueberry muffin (or a loaf cake—see also my recipe on page 48!): not too sweet and perfect for breakfast or dessert. Or lunch dessert—it's a thing.

MAKES 18 MUFFINS

2½ cups all-purpose flour

2½ teaspoons baking powder

½ teaspoon baking soda

½ teaspoon salt

½ cup unsalted butter, softened

1¼ cups granulated sugar

2 eggs

2 teaspoons vanilla extract

1 cup buttermilk

2 cups blueberries

2 tablespoons coarse sugar

Preheat the oven to 375°F and line 18 muffin cups with paper liners. In a bowl, whisk together the flour, baking powder, baking soda, and salt. In a large bowl, beat together the butter and granulated sugar until fluffy. Add the eggs and vanilla, and mix until well blended. Add the flour mixture and buttermilk in alternating additions, beginning and ending with the flour mixture, beating until well mixed before adding the next addition. Fold in the blueberries until they are evenly distributed.

Scoop the batter evenly into the muffin cups and sprinkle the tops with the coarse sugar. Bake until the tops are light golden brown, and a cake tester inserted into the center comes out clean, 20 to 25 minutes. Cool in the muffin pans before removing and serving.

ORANGE-POPPY SEED MUFFINS

Poppy seed muffins have always been one of my favorite types of muffins. This citrus variety is a bit unusual, offering a new take from its sister lemon flavor, but it makes sense to have a little orange juice with breakfast, right, folks?

Preheat the oven to 375°F and line 12 muffin cups with paper liners. In a large bowl, stir together the flour, granulated sugar, baking powder, and salt. In another bowl, whisk together the egg, milk, orange juice, melted butter, orange zest, vanilla, and orange extract, if using. Pour the egg mixture into the dry mixture. Stir together until just combined—do not overmix. Gently fold in the poppy seeds.

Evenly scoop the batter into the prepared muffin cups. Sprinkle the tops with coarse sugar. Bake until golden brown, 20 to 25 minutes. Cool slightly before serving.

MAKES 12 MUFFINS

2¼ cups all-purpose flour

¼ cup granulated sugar

2½ teaspoons baking powder

½ teaspoon salt

1 egg

½ cup whole milk

½ cup orange juice

¼ cup unsalted butter, melted

Finely grated zest of 1 orange

1 teaspoon vanilla extract

½ teaspoon orange extract (optional)

2 tablespoons poppy seeds

¼ cup coarse sugar

PUMPKIN-SPICE MUFFINS

There is one thing that my husband asks me to bake every time he has the chance—pumpkin muffins. I only ever make them in the fall, but here we are, it's fall. Or at least it will feel like fall when you bake up these autumn treats.

MAKES ABOUT 16 MUFFINS

FOR THE MUFFINS

2 cups all-purpose flour

1 teaspoon ground cinnamon

¾ teaspoon baking soda

½ teaspoon salt

½ teaspoon ground nutmeg

½ teaspoon ground ginger

¼ teaspoon ground allspice

⅛ teaspoon ground cloves

¾ cup granulated sugar

⅓ cup firmly packed brown sugar

½ cup vegetable oil

3 eggs

1 cup pumpkin puree

2 teaspoons vanilla extract

FOR THE CRUMBLE

6 tablespoons unsalted butter, melted

¾ cup all-purpose flour

½ cup firmly packed brown sugar

½ cup granulated sugar

1 teaspoon ground cinnamon

For the muffins: Preheat the oven to 375°F and line 16 muffin cups with paper liners. In a bowl, whisk together the flour, cinnamon, baking soda, salt, nutmeg, ginger, allspice, and cloves. In a large bowl, beat together the granulated sugar, brown sugar, and oil until combined. Add the eggs, pumpkin, and vanilla, and stir until combined. Slowly add the flour mixture, and beat until the batter is smooth. Fill each muffin cup about three-quarters full with the batter.

For the crumble: In a bowl, stir together the melted butter, flour, brown sugar, granulated sugar, and cinnamon until the mixture is crumbly. Sprinkle the top of each muffin cup with the crumb mixture, dividing evenly.

Bake until a cake tester inserted into the center of a muffin comes out clean, 20 to 22 minutes. These muffins can be enjoyed warm or completely cooled!

CRUMB CAKE

Crumb cake is the perfect brunch dish. It's not too sweet, the crumbs are super delicious, and it's great for dessert too. Lucky us. This one is full of cinnamon and topped with big hearty crumbs.

For the cake: Preheat the oven to 350°F, and grease and flour an 8-inch round cake pan. In a large bowl, beat together the butter and granulated sugar until light and fluffy. Beat in the eggs, vanilla, and sour cream. In a small bowl, whisk together the cake flour, baking powder, salt, and cinnamon. Add the flour mixture to the butter mixture and beat until well mixed. The batter will be thick. Spread the batter into your prepared pan.

For the crumb topping: In a bowl, stir together the cake flour, brown sugar, granulated sugar, cinnamon, salt, and melted butter until a crumb mixture forms. Evenly sprinkle the crumb mixture over the top of the cake batter, and press down gently.

Bake until a cake tester inserted into the center of the cake comes out clean, 35 to 38 minutes. Cool in the pan before removing. Cut into wedges and serve.

MAKES 8 TO 10 SERVINGS

FOR THE CAKE

½ cup unsalted butter, softened

¾ cup granulated sugar

2 eggs

2 teaspoons vanilla extract

¼ cup sour cream

1 cup cake flour

1 teaspoon baking powder

1 teaspoon salt

1 teaspoon ground cinnamon

FOR THE CRUMB TOPPING

2 cups cake flour

¾ cup firmly packed brown sugar

½ cup granulated sugar

½ teaspoon ground cinnamon

¼ teaspoon salt

¾ cup unsalted butter, melted

BANANA CRUMB BREAD

This banana bread is a twist on my grandma's traditional recipe. My mom has been using this recipe for years as well, and it's great with or without the crumb topping. I like to bake it in a cake pan instead of a loaf pan so it seems extra fancy.

MAKES 8 TO 10 SERVINGS

FOR THE BREAD

6 tablespoons unsalted butter, softened

¾ cup granulated sugar

2 eggs

1 cup mashed ripe banana

3 tablespoons water

1 teaspoon vanilla extract

2 cups all-purpose flour

1 teaspoon salt

¾ teaspoon baking soda

½ teaspoon ground cinnamon

¼ teaspoon ground nutmeg

½ cup chopped walnuts

FOR THE CRUMB TOPPING

¾ cup all-purpose flour

½ cup firmly packed brown sugar

½ cup old-fashioned oats

¼ cup chopped walnuts

6 tablespoons unsalted butter, melted

½ teaspoon ground cinnamon

¼ teaspoon salt

For the bread: Preheat the oven to 350°F, and grease and flour a 9-inch round cake pan. In a large bowl, beat together the softened butter and granulated sugar until smooth. Add the eggs, mashed banana, water, and vanilla and mix to combine. In another bowl, combine the flour, salt, baking soda, cinnamon, and nutmeg. Add the flour mixture to the butter mixture and beat until combined. Fold in the chopped walnuts, and pour the batter into your prepared pan, spreading it evenly.

For the crumb topping: In a bowl, mix the flour, brown sugar, oats, walnuts, melted butter, cinnamon, and salt together with a fork until medium crumbs form. If yours comes out too dry, add a teaspoon of water. If it's too wet, add a teaspoon of flour. Evenly sprinkle the crumb mixture over the top of the batter.

Bake for 40 minutes. Then place a piece of foil over the top to prevent overbrowning, and bake until a cake tester inserted into the center of the bread comes out clean, 10 to 15 minutes longer. Cool in the pan completely before removing. Cut into wedges and serve.

SWEET HONEY CORNBREAD

Cornbread is such a staple in my house. This recipe is simple and sweet, with some extra flavor from the black pepper. Since this recipe is pretty basic, you can add chopped jalapeños, cheddar cheese, or pretty much anything you like. It's also fantastic as is, served with butter and honey.

Preheat the oven to 375°F, and grease a 9-by-13-inch pan. In a bowl, whisk together the flour, cornmeal, baking powder, salt, and pepper. In a large bowl, beat together the vegetable oil and sugar until smooth. Add the eggs and honey, and beat until combined. Add the flour mixture and buttermilk in alternating additions, starting and ending with the flour mixture, and beating until completely mixed before adding the next addition.

Pour the batter into the prepared pan, and bake until a cake tester inserted into the center comes out clean, 28 to 30 minutes. Cool slightly, and cut into squares.

MAKES 12 SERVINGS

3 cups all-purpose flour

2 cups yellow cornmeal

1 tablespoon plus 1½ teaspoons baking powder

2 teaspoons salt

2 teaspoons freshly ground black pepper

⅔ cup vegetable oil

1 cup sugar

4 eggs

½ cup honey

2 cups buttermilk

CHOCOLATE–CHOCOLATE CHIP BREAD

Sometimes, quick breads are just loaf cakes with healthier names. This may be one of those times. This delicious loaf is studded with chocolate chunks, and flavored with the deep notes of espresso and cocoa. Bake it up when it's time to get your chocolate fix.

MAKES 8 TO 10 SERVINGS

1¾ cups cake flour

⅓ cup dark cocoa powder

1 teaspoon espresso powder

½ teaspoon baking powder

½ teaspoon salt

½ cup unsalted butter, softened

1¼ cups sugar

2 eggs

2 teaspoons vanilla extract

⅔ cup buttermilk

1 cup dark chocolate chips

Preheat the oven to 350°F, and grease and flour a 9-by-5-inch loaf pan. In a bowl, whisk together the cake flour, cocoa powder, espresso powder, baking powder, and salt. In a large bowl, beat together the butter and sugar until fluffy. Beat in the eggs and vanilla until smooth. Beat in the flour mixture and buttermilk in alternating additions, starting and ending with the flour mixture, beating until well mixed before adding the next addition. Stir in the chocolate chips. Spread the batter evenly in the prepared loaf pan.

Bake until a cake tester inserted into the center of the bread comes out clean, 60 to 65 minutes. Let cool completely in the pan on a wire rack before removing, and cut into slices to serve.

BANANA-ZUCCHINI BREAD

This recipe came about because my boss brought in a few zucchini from his garden to the office. At the end of the day, there was one left, and I snagged it because I knew I had some overripe bananas at home too. This bread is everything you want in a zucchini bread or a banana bread, so why not just combine them?

Preheat the oven to 350°F, and lightly grease and flour a 9-by-5-inch loaf pan. In a bowl, stir together the flour, cinnamon, baking powder, nutmeg, baking soda, and salt. In a large bowl, beat together the mashed banana, butter, and sugar until combined. Add the milk, eggs, and vanilla, and stir to combine. Slowly add in the flour mixture, and beat until completely incorporated. Fold in the grated zucchini. Pour the batter into your prepared loaf pan, spreading evenly.

Bake until a cake tester inserted into the center of the bread comes out clean, 55 to 60 minutes. Cool before removing from the pan. Cut into thick slices to serve.

MAKES 8 TO 10 SERVINGS

2½ cups all-purpose flour

2 teaspoons ground cinnamon

1¼ teaspoons baking powder

1 teaspoon ground nutmeg

½ teaspoon baking soda

½ teaspoon salt

1 large overripe banana, mashed

½ cup unsalted butter, softened

1 cup sugar

2 tablespoons whole milk

2 eggs

1 teaspoon vanilla extract

1 cup shredded zucchini

DOUBLE-BLUEBERRY LOAF CAKE

When blueberry muffins aren't enough, reach for this loaf.
It's packed with both fresh blueberries and blueberry pie filling,
resulting in the best loaf cake, like, ever.

MAKES 8 TO 10 SERVINGS

½ cup unsalted butter, softened

½ cup granulated sugar

2 eggs

¼ cup sour cream

¾ cup self-rising flour

¼ cup plus 2 teaspoons all-purpose
flour

½ teaspoon salt

2 tablespoons heavy cream

½ cup fresh blueberries

3 to 4 tablespoons purchased
blueberry pie filling

2 tablespoons coarse sugar

Preheat the oven to 350°F, and grease and flour a
9-by-5-inch loaf pan. In a bowl, beat together the
butter and granulated sugar until fluffy. Add the
eggs and sour cream and beat until combined.
Add the self-rising flour, ¼ cup of the all-purpose
flour, and the salt. Mix until combined—it will be
thick. Beat in the heavy cream.

In a bowl, toss the fresh blueberries with the
remaining 2 teaspoons all-purpose flour until
coated, and then fold into the batter. Spread about
half of the batter into the pan. Then take 1 to
2 tablespoons of the blueberry pie filling and drizzle
it into the batter. Using a butter knife, swirl the
pie filling into the batter, creating a mottled effect.
Spread the remaining batter over the top, drop
in the remaining pie filling, and swirl again.
Sprinkle the top with the coarse sugar.

Bake until a cake tester comes out clean, 50 to
60 minutes. Let cool completely on a wire rack
before removing from the pan. Slice and serve.

ESPRESSO POUND CAKE

Pound cakes are difficult to make at altitude—they often end up doughy and dense. This cake is the perfect balance, though it's not quite as traditional as some recipes you may have seen. Also, coffee, duh.

Preheat the oven to 350°F, and grease and flour an 8-by-4-inch loaf pan. In a small bowl, whisk together the cake flour, espresso powder, baking powder, and salt. In a large bowl, beat together the butter and sugar until fluffy. Beat in the eggs. In a small bowl, stir together the cooled espresso, cream, and vanilla. Add the flour mixture and the espresso mixture in alternating additions to the butter mixture, starting and ending with the flour mixture and beating well after each addition. Beat for several minutes, until the batter is very smooth.

Pour the batter into the prepared pan and bake until a cake tester inserted into the center of the cake comes out clean, 45 to 50 minutes. Let cool in the pan on a wire rack before removing, cut into slices, and enjoy!

MAKES ABOUT 8 SERVINGS

1½ cups cake flour

1 teaspoon espresso powder

½ teaspoon baking powder

½ teaspoon salt

6 tablespoons unsalted butter, softened

¾ cup plus 2 tablespoons sugar

2 eggs

¼ cup strongly brewed espresso, or ¼ cup hot water mixed with ½ teaspoon espresso powder, cooled

3 tablespoons heavy cream

1 teaspoon vanilla extract

MARBLE LOAF CAKE

This sweet swirl loaf cake is just what you need with your morning coffee. When you get to the swirling step, make sure to push your knife all the way to the bottom of the pan so you get that pretty swirl throughout.

MAKES 8 TO 10 SERVINGS

¼ cup dark cocoa powder

¼ cup boiling water

1½ cups cake flour

½ teaspoon baking powder

½ teaspoon salt

6 tablespoons unsalted butter, softened

1 cup sugar

2 eggs

⅓ cup whole milk

1 teaspoon vanilla extract

Preheat the oven to 350°F, and grease and flour a 9-by-5-inch loaf pan. In a small heatproof bowl, stir together the cocoa powder and boiling water. In a bowl, whisk together the cake flour, baking powder, and salt. In a large bowl, beat together the butter and sugar until fluffy. Add the eggs, milk, and vanilla, and stir until combined. Slowly add the flour mixture until combined.

Transfer about one-third of the batter to a small bowl and add the cocoa powder mixture, stirring until combined.

Scoop the vanilla and chocolate batters into the prepared loaf pan in alternating scoops. Using a knife, swirl the batters together to create a mottled effect. Bake until a cake tester inserted into the center of the cake comes out clean, 40 to 45 minutes. Let cool completely in the pan on a wire rack before removing. Cut into slices to serve.

BREADS, ROLLS & PIZZAS

CRUSTY HERB BREAD

This is my version of the popular no-knead Dutch oven bread originally developed by Jim Lahey, which has been modified for high altitude. The dough is very sticky and soft, and yet it creates a beautiful crusty round loaf of bread that will make you feel like you're walking the streets of Paris.

In a large bowl, stir together the flour, yeast, salt, rosemary, thyme, and pepper. Pour the warm water into the flour mixture. Stir together until the mixture is combined and there are no dry pockets of flour. It will be lumpy and thick. Cover the bowl with plastic wrap and let the dough rise in a warm place for 2 to 3 hours. The dough should have risen to double the size and will be flat on top, with many bubbles.

Preheat the oven to 425°F and place a 3.5-quart Dutch oven with the lid on into the oven while it preheats. Scrape out the dough onto a floured work surface. The dough will still be fairly wet. Using your hands and a kneading motion, slowly incorporate more flour, just enough so that you can shape the dough into a ball. The ball will still be very soft and will flatten some as you let it sit. Place the dough onto a sheet of parchment paper, and let it rest, uncovered, for 15 to 20 minutes.

Carefully remove the Dutch oven from the oven, and remove the lid. Place the parchment paper with the dough on it inside the pot. Replace the lid and bake for 45 minutes. Then remove the lid, and bake until golden, another 5 to 10 minutes. The bread will be very hot; cool slightly with the lid off, and cut into wedges to serve warm!

MAKES 1 ROUND LOAF

- 3½ cups all-purpose flour, plus more for working the dough
- 1¼ teaspoons active dry yeast
- 2 teaspoons salt
- 1 teaspoon ground dried rosemary
- 1 teaspoon ground dried thyme
- ½ teaspoon freshly ground black pepper
- 1¾ cup warm water (between 100°F and 110°F)

BREAD RING WITH PESTO BUTTER

I like the idea of making bread in a ring pan to make smaller pieces to snack on. Also, it's a lot of bread, and you're gonna need some fancy butter to go with it—I've got just the thing here.

MAKES 1 BREAD RING

FOR THE BREAD

4½ teaspoons active dry yeast

½ cup warm water (between 100°F and 110°F)

2 tablespoons sugar

1 cup plus 2 tablespoons whole milk

1 cup water

2 tablespoons vegetable oil

2 teaspoons salt

1 teaspoon freshly ground black pepper

1 teaspoon garlic powder

5 to 5½ cups bread flour, plus more for working the dough

For the bread: In a small bowl, mix together the yeast, warm water, and sugar, and let stand until foamy, about 5 minutes. Meanwhile, in a small saucepan, heat 1 cup of the milk, the water, oil, salt, pepper, and garlic powder until it reads about 120°F on an instant-read thermometer. Pour the milk mixture into the bowl of a stand mixer fitted with the paddle attachment or a large bowl. Add 4 cups of the flour, and beat together with the mixer or a wooden spoon until combined. Add the yeast mixture, and beat together for several minutes. You will have a lumpy, very wet mixture at this point. Add another ½ cup of flour, and beat together. Continue slowly adding flour until the dough leaves the sides of the bowl and is no longer sticky. Pull the dough out onto a floured work surface and gently knead in a little more flour until it's smooth. Place the dough into a lightly oiled bowl and cover with plastic wrap.

Set the dough aside in a warm place and let it rise until just less than doubled in size, 50 to 55 minutes. Punch down the dough, and knead on a floured surface once or twice. Place the dough back in the bowl, cover, and let it rest again until it rises by about one-third in size, 40 to 45 minutes.

Lightly grease a 10-inch tube pan. Pat the dough into a large rectangle and roll it into a log. Pinch the seam closed, form the dough into a ring, and pinch to seal the seam. Place the dough into the prepared pan and cover with plastic wrap. Preheat the oven to 400°F. Let

the dough rise again for a final 20 minutes while the oven preheats. When the oven is ready, brush the top of the dough with the remaining 2 tablespoons milk. Bake for 15 minutes and then reduce the temperature to 375°F. Continue baking until golden brown and the inside of the bread registers 190°F to 195°F on an instant-read thermometer, about 30 minutes. Remove from the pan immediately and cool on a wire rack.

For the pesto butter: Using an electric mixer, mix together the butter, pesto, roasted garlic, garlic powder, salt, and pepper until the mixture is light and fluffy.

Cut the bread ring into wedges and serve with the pesto butter.

FOR THE PESTO BUTTER

1 cup unsalted butter, softened

2 tablespoons pesto of your choice

1 tablespoon roasted garlic (see page 24)

½ teaspoon garlic powder

½ teaspoon salt

½ teaspoon freshly ground black pepper

VANILLA-SCENTED BRIOCHE

Brioche is my favorite kind of bread. It's buttery and dense, and this
version has a light vanilla flavor. You can shape this dough however
you'd like, but braiding is a classic method. This is a great loaf to
slice up and use for French toast or bread pudding!

In a small saucepan, combine the milk, vanilla bean
paste or seeds, and vanilla extract, and warm over
low heat until it reaches 115°F on an instant-read
thermometer. In the bowl of a stand mixer fitted
with the paddle attachment, or in a large bowl using
a wooden spoon, mix together the warmed milk
mixture and yeast. Add the sugar, 2 of the eggs,
and the melted butter, and stir together. Add the
bread flour and salt. Mix together until the dough
becomes smooth and all the flour is incorporated.
At this stage, the dough will still be rather sticky to
the touch. Take the dough out of the bowl, and place
onto a floured work surface. Knead the dough, slowly
adding more flour as needed, for about 5 minutes.
The dough will still be a bit tacky to the touch, but
less so than when it was removed from the bowl. Place
the dough in a large buttered bowl, and cover with
plastic wrap or a clean dishtowel. Let the dough rise
in a warm place until it has nearly doubled in size.
For me, this takes about 30 to 40 minutes. The timing
here is a guideline, but be sure to keep your eye on
the dough!

Put the dough on the work surface and knead it once
or twice, and return it to the bowl, covering again.
Place the dough in the refrigerator to rise a second
time, allowing it to increase in size by roughly one-
third. Keep in mind that chilling the dough slows the

MAKES 1 LOAF

⅓ cup plus 1 tablespoon whole milk

2 teaspoons vanilla bean paste, or
the seeds scraped from 1 whole
vanilla bean

1 teaspoon vanilla extract

1 tablespoon active dry yeast

3 tablespoons sugar

3 eggs

¼ cup unsalted butter, melted

2 cups bread flour, plus more for
working the dough

1 teaspoon salt

Butter and strawberry or raspberry
jam for serving

CONTINUED ON NEXT PAGE

rising process. This second rise should take about 1 hour, but be sure to keep an eye on the dough.

Remove the risen dough from the refrigerator, and let it rest at room temperature for 20 minutes.

Cut the dough into 3 even sections. Roll each section into a rope that is roughly ¾ inch thick. Pinch the 3 pieces together at one end, and then braid the strands together. Pinch together the pieces when you reach the end of the braid, and then tuck both ends under the loaf.

Preheat the oven to 400°F and grease a 9-by-5-inch loaf pan. Take a small baking pan (I use an 8-inch-square cake pan) and fill it about halfway with water. Place it on the lower rack inside the oven, off to the side. Leave this pan of water in the oven while baking the brioche. Place the dough braid into the prepared loaf pan, and cover lightly with plastic wrap while the oven preheats—this is the third rise, and you should only see a slight change in size during the roughly 15 to 20 minutes it will take to preheat the oven.

Beat the remaining egg, and brush it generously on the top of the braid. Bake the loaf until the top is golden (the egg wash will also give it a nice sheen), 35 to 40 minutes. Let cool completely in the pan before removing, and cut into slices to serve with butter and jam!

PARMESAN–BLACK PEPPER BRIOCHE

I like sweet swirl breads as much as anyone, but putting Parmesan cheese and black pepper into brioche is something magical, you guys. This bread is best served lightly toasted, to melt the cheese, and with a little butter spread on top!

In a small saucepan, warm the milk over low heat until it reads 115°F on an instant-read thermometer. In the bowl of a stand mixer fitted with the paddle attachment, or in a large bowl with a wooden spoon, mix together the warm milk and yeast. Add the sugar, 2 of the eggs, and the melted butter, and mix to combine. Add 1 cup of the bread flour and the salt. Mix until the dough becomes smooth, adding the all-purpose flour and remaining ½ cup bread flour if necessary. At this stage, the dough will still be rather sticky to the touch. Take the dough out of the bowl, and place on a floured work surface. Knead the dough, slowly adding more flour as needed, for about 5 minutes. The dough will still be a bit tacky to the touch, but less so than when it was removed from the bowl. Place the dough in a large buttered bowl, and cover with plastic wrap or a clean dishtowel. Let the dough rise in a warm place until it has nearly doubled in size. For me, this takes about 30 to 40 minutes. The timing here is a guideline, but be sure to keep your eye on the dough!

Put the dough on the work surface and knead it once or twice, and return it to the bowl, covering with plastic wrap again. Place the dough in the refrigerator, allowing it to increase in size by roughly one-third. Keep in mind that chilling the dough slows the rising process. This second rise should take about 1 hour, but be sure to keep an eye on the dough.

CONTINUED ON NEXT PAGE

MAKES 1 LOAF

⅓ cup plus 1 tablespoon whole milk

1 tablespoon active dry yeast

3 tablespoons sugar

3 eggs

¼ cup unsalted butter, melted

1 to 1½ cups bread flour

1 teaspoon salt

½ cup all-purpose flour, plus more for working the dough

½ cup unsalted butter, softened

¾ cup grated Parmesan cheese

1½ tablespoons freshly ground black pepper

PARMESAN-BLACK PEPPER BRIOCHE
(CON'T)

Remove the risen dough from the refrigerator, and let it rest at room temperature for 20 minutes.

Lightly grease an 8-by-4-inch or 9-by-5-inch loaf pan. Place the dough on a lightly floured work surface. Using a rolling pin, roll the dough into a rectangle, about 18 inches long and 8 or 9 inches wide (to fit inside your loaf pan). Spread the softened butter evenly across the rectangle, all the way to the edges. Evenly sprinkle the grated Parmesan and black pepper over the top. Beginning at a short end, roll the dough into a snug log and place it in the prepared pan.

Preheat the oven to 400°F. Take a small baking pan (I use an 8-inch-square cake pan) and fill it about halfway with water. Place it on the lower rack inside the oven, off to the side. Leave this pan of water in the oven while baking the brioche. Cover the loaf with plastic wrap and set it aside to rise while the oven preheats—this is the third rise, and you should only see a slight change in size during the roughly 15 to 20 minutes it will take to preheat the oven.

Beat the remaining egg, and brush it generously on the top of the loaf. Bake the loaf until the top is golden (the egg wash will also give it a nice sheen), 35 to 40 minutes. Let cool, slightly or completely, in the pan on a wire rack before removing, and cut into slices to serve.

POPPY SEED BURGER BUNS

Fresh bread is, like, from the heavens, and these homemade buns are no exception. I sprinkle mine with poppy seeds, but you can use sesame seeds, dried onion flakes, or whatever combo fits your fancy.

In a saucepan, warm the milk, water, melted butter, and honey until it reads between 100°F and 110°F on an instant-read thermometer. Remove from the heat, stir in the yeast, and let stand until foamy, about 5 minutes.

In a large bowl, or the bowl of a stand mixer fitted with the paddle attachment, stir together 1 of the eggs and the salt. Add the milk mixture and stir until combined. Add the flour, 1 cup at a time, stirring between each addition, until all the flour has been added and the mixture is slightly sticky. Scrape the dough out onto a lightly floured work surface, and knead 5 to 10 times, until the dough is smooth and no longer sticky. Place the dough in a lightly oiled large bowl. Cover with plastic wrap and let rise in a warm place until the dough has doubled in size, 20 to 30 minutes. Keep an eye on the dough—you do not want to it to rise too much.

Preheat the oven to 375°F, and line a large baking sheet with parchment paper or a nonstick mat. Divide the dough into 8 even sections. Fold in the corners of each dough section to create a smooth, round top, and then roll each one into a ball using the palms of your hands. Evenly space the dough balls on the baking sheet, and cover with plastic wrap. Let them rest until they have risen by about another third, 10 to 15 minutes.

Beat the remaining egg and generously brush it over the rolls. Sprinkle with the poppy seeds. Bake the rolls until rich golden brown, 15 to 20 minutes. Cool, slice crosswise, and enjoy.

MAKES 8 BUNS

1 cup whole milk

1 cup water

½ cup unsalted butter, melted

3 tablespoons honey

2 tablespoons active dry yeast

2 eggs

2 teaspoons salt

5½ cups bread flour

2 teaspoons poppy seeds

PRETZEL TWISTS

These are the classic soft pretzels we all grew up with, but made at home. There are a few steps involved here, but you'll be surprised how much these want to be dipped in melted cheese when you're finished!

MAKES 16 TWISTS

1½ cups warm water (about 125°F)

6 tablespoons unsalted butter, melted

2 tablespoons firmly packed brown sugar

2¼ teaspoons (1 packet) active dry yeast

4½ to 5 cups all-purpose flour

2½ teaspoons table salt

¼ cup baking soda (that's right, a whole quarter cup!)

1 egg, beaten with a little water

Coarse salt and freshly ground black pepper

In the bowl of a stand mixer fitted with the paddle attachment, or a large bowl, mix together the warm water, melted butter, brown sugar, and yeast. Let stand until the mixture is foamy, about 5 minutes. Meanwhile, in another bowl, mix together 4½ cups of the flour and the table salt. Add the flour mixture to the yeast mixture and mix with the stand mixer or a wooden spoon until the dough pulls away from the sides of the bowl. The dough shouldn't be too sticky, so use more flour if needed. Transfer the dough to a floured work surface and knead until smooth and uniform, about 5 minutes. Form the dough into a ball. Lightly grease a bowl with oil. Toss the dough in the bowl, flipping to oil the top. Loosely cover with plastic wrap, and let the dough rise in a warm place until it has doubled in size, 30 to 60 minutes.

Preheat the oven to 425°F. In a large pot, bring 2 quarts of water to a boil. Quickly add the baking soda—be careful, it might splatter! Line 2 baking sheets with parchment paper or nonstick mats. Divide the dough into 16 equal pieces. Roll each piece into a rope, then fold it in half and twist, and fold the ends of the twisted rope into the loop on the top to create a twisted roll shape. Using a slotted spoon, put the twists in the boiling water 4 at a time, for about 30 seconds each. Transfer the boiled twists to the prepared sheet pans. Brush the twists with the beaten egg mixture and immediately sprinkle with coarse salt and pepper.

Bake until the twists are golden brown, 12 to 15 minutes. Serve warm.

CHOCOLATE LOAF BREAD

While you might be expecting a cake-like quick bread when it comes to a chocolate loaf, this version is a sweet twist on the pillowy yeast breads you know. You want the best French toast of your life? Make it with this bread. Seriously.

In a small bowl, stir together the warm water, sugar, and yeast, and set aside until foamy, 5 to 10 minutes. Meanwhile, in a large bowl, stir together ½ cup of the milk, the water, and the oil. Stir in the yeast mixture. Add the bread flour, cocoa powder, and salt and stir until the dough comes together. On a floured work surface, knead the dough until it is fairly smooth, 5 to 10 minutes. Place the dough into a lightly greased bowl, and allow it to rise in a warm place until roughly doubled in size, about 45 minutes.

Lightly grease a 9-by-5-inch loaf pan. Put the dough on a floured work surface and use a rolling pin to roll into a ½-inch-thick rectangle. Sprinkle the chocolate chunks over the rectangle and press them into the dough. Starting on a shorter side, roll the dough into a tight log. Place the log in your prepared pan and cover with plastic wrap. Let the dough rest for about 30 minutes. After about 10 minutes of rising, preheat the oven to 375°F.

Brush the top of the dough with the remaining 2 tablespoons milk. Bake until the loaf looks dry, feels solid if you tap it with a spoon, and an instant-read thermometer registers 190°F when inserted into the center of the loaf, 45 to 50 minutes. Let cool in the pan for 15 to 20 minutes before removing, and cut into slices to serve warm.

MAKES 1 LOAF

¼ cup warm water (about 115°F)

2 tablespoons sugar

1 tablespoon active dry yeast

½ cup plus 2 tablespoons whole milk

½ cup water

1 tablespoon vegetable oil

2¼ cups bread flour

¼ cup dark cocoa powder

1 teaspoon salt

5 ounces chocolate chunks

CHOCOLATE BABKA

Babka is something I first tasted in New York, and it's one of the best bread recipes in the world as far as I'm concerned. Once baked, it looks very complicated and beautiful, but it's actually quite simple to make.

MAKES 1 LOAF

FOR THE DOUGH

⅓ cup whole milk

3 tablespoons granulated sugar

1 teaspoon vanilla extract

1 tablespoon active dry yeast

2½ to 2¾ cups bread flour, plus more for working the dough

1½ teaspoons salt

1 teaspoon ground cinnamon

½ teaspoon espresso powder

2 eggs

¼ cup unsalted butter, melted

FOR THE FILLING

6 tablespoons unsalted butter

4 ounces dark chocolate, chopped

⅓ cup powdered sugar

3 tablespoons dark cocoa powder

¼ teaspoon salt

¼ teaspoon espresso powder

¼ cup semisweet mini chocolate chips

Powdered sugar for dusting (optional)

For the dough: In a small saucepan, warm the milk over low heat until it reads 115°F on an instant-read thermometer. Remove from the heat and stir in the granulated sugar, vanilla, and yeast. Set aside until foamy, 5 to 10 minutes.

In a bowl, stir together 2½ cups of the bread flour with the salt, cinnamon, and espresso powder. In a large bowl, stir together the eggs and melted butter. Add the yeast mixture and stir to mix. Add the flour mixture, and stir until a dough has formed. Turn the dough out onto a floured work surface. Knead the dough, adding more flour as needed, for about 5 minutes.

The dough will be fairly stiff. Generously butter a large bowl, add the dough, and cover with plastic wrap. Let the dough rise in a warm place until it has doubled in size. For me, this takes about 45 minutes to 1 hour, but you should keep a close eye on the dough after 30 minutes. Do not let the dough rise to more than double in size.

For the filling: In a small saucepan over low heat, melt together the butter and the chocolate. Whisk in the powdered sugar, cocoa powder, salt, and espresso powder. Set aside.

Remove the dough from the bowl, and place it on a floured work surface. Using a floured rolling pin, begin to roll out the dough. You want the dough to be

CONTINUED ON NEXT PAGE

very thin, ⅛ to ¼ inch thick, and in the shape of a large rectangle. Since the dough will be a bit elastic, this may take some working.

Using an offset spatula, spread the filling evenly on the rolled-out dough, spreading it all the way to the edges. Evenly sprinkle the mini chocolate chips on top of the filling.

Line a baking sheet with parchment paper or a non-stick sheet. Starting at one of the short sides, begin to roll up the dough, very tightly, like you would a cinnamon roll. Once you have the dough completely rolled up, slice the roll in half lengthwise. Twist the two halves together, lightly pinching each end together. Form the roll into a round, pinching the ends together, and place on your prepared baking sheet. Cover with plastic wrap.

Preheat the oven to 375°F and let the dough rest for 25 to 30 minutes. The dough should rise during this time just slightly, by about one-third at most. Bake the dough uncovered until deep golden brown and an instant-read thermometer inserted in the center of the loaf reads 165°F to 170°F, 40 to 45 minutes. If you notice the bread becoming too brown on top, cover the pan with foil for the remaining baking time. Remove from the oven, and let cool completely in the pan on a wire rack. Dust with powdered sugar, if you like, cut into slices, and enjoy!

COZY CINNAMON ROLLS

When you've had a long week and need an indulgent Sunday treat, make these. When you want to make a guest feel at home, make these. When you want to put smiles on faces at breakfast or lunch or dessert, make these. These classic, sweet rolls, topped with generous amounts of cream cheese frosting, will warm your soul.

For the rolls: In a saucepan over low heat, warm the milk until it reads 120°F on an instant-read thermometer. Remove from the heat and stir in the granulated sugar, vanilla, and yeast. Set aside until foamy, 5 to 10 minutes. In a large bowl, stir together the eggs and ½ cup of the butter. The mixture will be lumpy. Add the yeast mixture and stir until combined. Stir in the salt, and then add the bread flour, 2 cups at a time, mixing between additions, until you reach 5 cups. Place the dough onto a generously floured work surface and knead in the remaining ½ cup or so of flour. The dough will be fairly sturdy. Place the dough into a lightly buttered bowl and cover with plastic wrap. Set the dough aside in a warm place until it has risen by about one-third, about 30 minutes.

In a bowl, stir together the brown sugar and cinnamon. Set aside. Put the dough on a lightly floured work surface. Using a rolling pin, roll the dough into a very large rectangle, about ¼ to ½ inch thick. Spread the remaining ½ cup butter evenly across the dough all the way to the edges. Sprinkle the brown sugar and cinnamon mixture over the entire rectangle, gently pressing it into the butter and dough so it's fairly packed into it.

CONTINUED ON NEXT PAGE

MAKES 16 FROSTED ROLLS

FOR THE ROLLS

1½ cups whole milk

½ cup granulated sugar

1 teaspoon vanilla extract

1 tablespoon plus 1 teaspoon active dry yeast

2 eggs

1 cup unsalted butter, softened

1 teaspoon salt

5 to 5½ cups bread flour, plus more for working the dough

1½ cups firmly packed brown sugar

3½ tablespoons ground cinnamon

COZY CINNAMON ROLLS (CON'T)

This will keep everything in place for each roll. Starting on one of the long sides, begin to tightly roll the dough into a log. Work slowly, and make sure you are rolling the dough nice and tight. Cut off any uneven edges on the log. Then cut the log in half, cut each of those halves in half, and so on until you have 16 evenly sized rolls. Place your rolls on a large baking sheet lined with parchment paper or a nonstick sheet, and cover with plastic wrap. Preheat the oven to 375°F. Meanwhile, let the rolls rise until they have just puffed and are touching on the edges, about 20 minutes. This should be about the amount of time it takes to heat the oven. Bake the rolls until they are golden brown, 12 to 15 minutes.

For the frosting: In a bowl, beat together the cream cheese, powdered sugar, vanilla, and salt until smooth. Add the milk and beat until smooth.

Top each roll generously with the frosting while they are still warm, and serve.

FOR THE FROSTING

1 package (8 ounces) cream cheese, softened

1½ cups powdered sugar

1 teaspoon vanilla extract

¼ teaspoon salt

1 tablespoon whole milk

CHOCOLATE CHIP CINNAMON ROLLS

These cinnamon rolls aren't far off from the classic, honestly,
but mini chocolate chips make a tasty addition.
Plus cinnamon rolls are maybe the best food in the entire world.

MAKES 15 TO 18 ROLLS

FOR THE ROLLS

½ cup warm water (between 100°F and 110°F)

2 tablespoons granulated sugar

4½ teaspoons (2 packets) active dry yeast

1 cup whole milk

1 cup water

2 tablespoons vegetable oil

2 teaspoons salt

2 teaspoons vanilla extract

5 to 5½ cups bread flour, plus more for working the dough

1¼ cups firmly packed brown sugar

3½ tablespoons ground cinnamon

½ cup unsalted butter, softened

¾ cup semisweet mini chocolate chips

For the rolls: In a small bowl, mix together the warm water, granulated sugar, and yeast, and set aside until foamy, about 5 minutes. Meanwhile, in a small saucepan over low heat, heat the milk, 1 cup water, oil, salt, and vanilla until the mixture reads 120°F on an instant-read thermometer. Pour the milk mixture into a stand mixer fitted with the paddle attachment, or a large bowl using a wooden spoon. Add 4 cups of the bread flour, and beat together until combined. Add the yeast mixture and beat for several minutes. You will have a very wet, lumpy mixture at this point. Mix in another ½ cup of flour, and beat until smooth. Continue slowly adding flour until the dough leaves the sides of the bowl and is no longer sticky. Pull the dough out onto a floured work surface and gently knead in a little more flour until it's smooth. Place the dough into a lightly oiled bowl, and cover with plastic wrap.

Let the dough rise in a warm place until it has doubled in size, 50 to 55 minutes. Punch down the dough and knead it once or twice on a floured surface. Place the dough back in the bowl, cover, and let it rest again until it has risen by about one-third, 40 to 45 minutes.

In a bowl, stir together the brown sugar and cinnamon and set aside. Put the dough on a lightly floured work surface. Using a rolling pin, roll out the dough into a large rectangle about ¼ to ½ inch thick. Spread the butter evenly across the dough all the way to the edges. Sprinkle the brown sugar–cinnamon mixture over the top and pat it down into the butter

and dough. Sprinkle the mini chocolate chips across the dough. Starting from a long side, roll up the dough tightly and evenly, and slice into 15 to 18 rolls. Place your rolls cut-side down on a greased baking sheet. Preheat the oven to 375°F. Let the rolls rise for another 15 minutes or so while the oven heats.

Bake until the rolls are golden brown, 30 to 35 minutes.

For the frosting: In a bowl, beat together the cream cheese, powdered sugar, milk, and vanilla until smooth.

Let the rolls cool for about 15 minutes. Smear the frosting over each roll, and serve.

FOR THE FROSTING

4 ounces cream cheese, softened

2 cups powdered sugar

1 tablespoon whole milk

1 teaspoon vanilla extract

DINNER ROLLS

Perfecting the art of dinner rolls has long been a goal of mine,
and I've managed it with this simple recipe. You'll end up with buttery,
cloud-like rolls that are not too dense, and not too yeasty in flavor.

In a saucepan, warm 2 cups of the milk, the melted butter, and the sugar until it reads between 100°F and 110°F on an instant-read thermometer. Remove from the heat, stir in the yeast, and let stand until foamy, about 5 minutes.

In a large bowl, or the bowl of a stand mixer fitted with the paddle attachment, stir together the egg and salt. Add the milk mixture and stir until combined. Add the bread flour, 1 cup at a time, stirring between each addition. Once you've added all 5 cups, the dough should still be slightly sticky. Scrape the dough out of the bowl and onto a floured work surface. Using your hands, knead the dough 5 to 10 times, or until it is smooth and no longer sticky. Place the dough in a lightly oiled large bowl and cover with plastic wrap. Set the dough aside in a warm place until just doubled in size, keeping a close eye on it, 20 to 25 minutes.

Preheat the oven to 375°F and line a baking sheet with parchment paper or a nonstick mat. Divide the dough into 20 even sections. Using the palms of your hands, roll each section into a ball, tucking in any corners so you end up with a smooth top. Place the rolls on your baking sheet—there should be room between each roll for rising. Cover the rolls with plastic wrap and allow them to rise until the oven is preheated, 10 to 15 minutes longer. The dough should rise by about another third. Brush the tops with the remaining 2 tablespoons milk. Bake until the rolls are golden brown, 12 to 15 minutes. Serve warm.

MAKES 20 ROLLS

2 cups plus 2 tablespoons whole milk

⅓ cup unsalted butter, melted

3 tablespoons sugar

2 tablespoons active dry yeast

1 egg

2 teaspoons salt

5 cups bread flour, plus more
for working the dough

PIZZA DOUGH

Use this dough for any pizza your heart desires, or omit the pepper, oregano, and basil to use it to make the cheesecake-stuffed monkey bread on page 90. Or garlic bread, or garlic knots, or whatever. It's all gonna be tasty.

MAKES ENOUGH DOUGH FOR 1 LARGE PIZZA

1 cup warm water (between 110°F and 115°F)

1 tablespoon active dry yeast

1½ teaspoons sugar

2 to 2½ cups all-purpose flour

½ teaspoon salt

½ teaspoon freshly ground black pepper

1 teaspoon dried oregano

½ teaspoon dried basil

In a large bowl, stir together the warm water, yeast, and sugar. Let the mixture sit and bloom until foamy, 5 minutes. Stir in 2 cups of the flour, and the salt, pepper, oregano, and basil until the dough starts to come together. Add more flour as needed until the dough becomes dry and smooth. Cover, and let the dough rest in a warm place for 20 minutes. To make the pizza, follow the recipes on pages 85 and 86. If you like, experiment with the toppings of your choice.

VARIATION: GARLIC KNOTS

Preheat the oven to 400°F. Line a baking sheet with parchment paper or a nonstick mat. Evenly divide the pizza dough into 16 pieces. On a lightly floured surface, roll each piece into a rope about 6 inches long, and tie each rope into a knot, tucking the ends underneath if needed. Place onto your baking sheet, evenly spaced. It's okay if they end up touching some when they bake. In a small bowl, stir together 6 large cloves minced garlic and 2 tablespoons olive oil. Brush evenly over the tops of all your rolls, making sure to get those chunks of garlic over the top. Bake the knots until they have puffed up and become golden brown on top, about 10 to 12 minutes. Serve warm. Makes 16 knots.

SPINACH-ARTICHOKE PIZZA

This is probably my favorite homemade pizza. It's kind of like making spinach-artichoke dip, and then spreading it all over a pizza crust and baking it. And it's pretty dang good.

Preheat the oven to 450°F and brush a large baking sheet with olive oil. In a large skillet over medium heat, cook the diced onion in the olive oil until the onions are soft and starting to caramelize, 5 to 10 minutes. Add the garlic and spinach, and stir until wilted. Add the cream cheese, sour cream, pesto, ½ teaspoon of the salt, and the pepper. Stir together until the cheese has melted completely. Stir in the artichokes and remove from the heat.

Place the dough on the baking sheet. Using your hands, gently press your dough to spread it out on your baking sheet to your desired thickness and size. Remember that the dough will rise some during baking.

Spread the spinach–cream cheese mixture evenly over the pizza, leaving room for a crust, and sprinkle the mozzarella cheese over the top.

In a small bowl, mix together the melted butter, garlic powder, oregano, and ½ teaspoon salt. Brush the mixture over the crust of the pizza. Bake until the pizza is golden brown and bubbling, 15 to 20 minutes. Let cool slightly, then cut into slices and serve.

MAKES 1 LARGE PIZZA

½ onion, diced

3 tablespoons olive oil

4 cloves garlic, minced

1 package (5 ounces) baby spinach

1 package (8 ounces) cream cheese

½ cup sour cream

2 tablespoons basil pesto

1 teaspoon salt

½ teaspoon freshly ground black pepper

½ cup chopped and drained canned artichokes

1 batch Pizza Dough (see page 82)

1 cup shredded mozzarella cheese

2 tablespoons unsalted butter, melted

½ teaspoon garlic powder

½ teaspoon dried oregano

PEPPERONI-ROMA TOMATO PIZZA

This is your classic pepperoni pizza, but with the addition of sliced tomatoes on top. It's everything you want in a pizza—crunchy, cheesy, greasy.

MAKES 1 LARGE PIZZA

Olive oil, for brushing

1 batch Pizza Dough (see page 82)

¼ cup pizza sauce of your choice

1½ cups shredded mozzarella cheese

3 tablespoons grated Parmesan cheese

1 Roma tomato, thinly sliced

20 pepperoni slices

2 tablespoons unsalted butter, melted

½ teaspoon garlic powder

½ teaspoon salt

½ teaspoon dried oregano

Preheat the oven to 450°F and brush a large baking sheet with olive oil. Place the dough on the baking sheet. Using your hands, gently press your dough to spread it out on your baking sheet to your desired thickness and size. Remember that the dough will rise some during baking. Spread the pizza sauce evenly over the dough, leaving room for a crust on the edge. Sprinkle the mozzarella and Parmesan cheeses evenly over the sauce, and then arrange the tomato and pepperoni slices over the top.

In a small bowl, mix together the melted butter, garlic powder, salt, and oregano. Brush the mixture over the crust of the pizza. Bake the pizza until golden and bubbling, 15 to 20 minutes. Let cool slightly, then cut into slices and serve.

TOMATO-GARLIC FOCACCIA

This super-easy bread is like a light pizza once you've got the tomato slices on it. It looks beautiful and makes a great side dish on pasta night.

In the bowl of a stand mixer fitted with the dough hook, or in a large bowl with a spatula or wooden spoon, mix together the water, milk, sugar, and yeast and let it stand until foamy, 5 to 10 minutes. Add the flour, olive oil, and table salt, and mix until the dough comes together. Add more flour as needed—the dough should be slightly sticky. Turn out the dough onto a floured work surface and knead a couple of times by hand. Place in a lightly oiled bowl and cover with plastic wrap. Leave in a warm place to rise until doubled in size, about 1 hour.

Divide the dough in half, and place each piece on an oiled baking sheet. Drizzle a little bit of olive oil on top of each piece and use your fingers to spread out each dough piece until each one is about ½ inch thick. The dough will be dimpled rather than smooth. Cover and let the dough rest until it has risen again by about a quarter, 20 to 30 minutes. Preheat the oven to 450°F.

Squeeze the roasted garlic out of its skin. Using the back of a spoon, mash the roasted garlic. Divide the roasted garlic paste over each loaf, and then layer on your sliced tomatoes, dividing evenly. Sprinkle the tops with coarse sea salt and pepper. Bake until golden brown, 15 minutes. Cut into rectangles and serve warm.

MAKES 2 LARGE LOAVES

¾ cup warm water (between 105°F and 110°F)

2 tablespoons whole milk, warmed (between 105°F and 110°F)

2 teaspoons sugar

1¼ teaspoons active dry yeast

2¼ cups all-purpose flour, plus more as needed

2 tablespoons olive oil, plus more for drizzling

1 teaspoon table salt

1 head roasted garlic (see page 24)

2 to 3 Roma tomatoes, thinly sliced

Coarse sea salt and freshly ground black pepper

STUFFED MONKEY BREAD

This recipe is a bit labor intensive, but the results are incredible. It's cheesecake-stuffed monkey bread, you guys—what could possibly be bad about that?

MAKES 12 TO 16 SERVINGS

1 package (8 ounces) cream cheese, softened

1¼ cups granulated sugar

3 teaspoons vanilla extract

1 cup unsalted butter

1 tablespoon ground cinnamon

1½ batches Pizza Dough (see page 82), omitting the pepper, oregano, and basil

About ¼ cup dark chocolate chips, or as needed

½ cup chopped hazelnuts

½ cup firmly packed brown sugar

½ teaspoon salt

Preheat the oven to 350°F and thoroughly spray a 10-cup Bundt pan with cooking spray. In a small bowl, beat together the cream cheese, ½ cup of the granulated sugar, and 2 teaspoons of the vanilla. Set aside. Melt ½ cup of the butter and place in another small bowl and let it cool. In a third small bowl, mix together the remaining ¾ cup granulated sugar and the cinnamon. Set aside.

Pull off a small piece of dough, about the size of a golf ball. Stretch the dough into a flat circle. Spoon a small amount of the cream cheese mixture in the center and add 2 chocolate chips. Stretch the dough around the filling back into a ball and pinch the seam to seal. Turn the ball into the melted butter to coat, and then roll in the cinnamon-sugar mixture. Place in the Bundt pan. Repeat the filling and coating steps until you have one layer of filled dough balls in the pan. Sprinkle half of the chopped hazelnuts over the top. Finish filling and rolling the rest of the dough balls. The pan should be about three-quarters full. Sprinkle the remaining hazelnuts over the top.

In a small saucepan, melt the remaining ½ cup butter, then whisk in the brown sugar, remaining 1 teaspoon vanilla, and the salt. Pour the mixture over the dough balls. Bake until the dough is set and the top is golden, 40 to 50 minutes. If the top starts to get too dark, cover the pan with foil and continue to bake.

Let cool for 10 to 15 minutes, then turn out onto a plate and enjoy warm. Simply pull off pieces of the bread to eat—it's messy, but delicious!

CAKES & CUPCAKES

TRIPLE-CHOCOLATE BUNDT CAKE

I first made this Bundt cake for my dad's birthday—he really likes
Bundt cakes! Why stop at just chocolate cake, when you can
fill it with ganache, top it with ganache, and add chocolate chips?

MAKES 10 TO 12 SERVINGS

FOR THE CAKE

2⅓ cups all-purpose flour

½ cup dark cocoa powder

1 teaspoon baking soda

½ teaspoon salt

½ cup unsalted butter, softened

1½ cups sugar

2 eggs

1 teaspoon vanilla extract

1½ cups plus 3 tablespoons
   buttermilk

FOR THE GANACHE

1 cup heavy cream

1 teaspoon vanilla extract

¼ teaspoon salt

1⅓ cups dark chocolate chips

Mini chocolate chips for sprinkling

For the cake: Preheat the oven to 375°F, and
generously grease and flour a 10-inch Bundt pan.
In a bowl, whisk together the flour, cocoa powder,
baking soda, and salt. In a large bowl, beat together
the butter and sugar until fluffy. Beat in the eggs
and vanilla. Add the buttermilk and flour mixture
in alternating additions, and mix until completely
incorporated between additions. Pour the batter into
the prepared Bundt pan, and set aside.

For the ganache: In a small saucepan over low heat,
combine the cream, vanilla, and salt and bring to a
simmer. Place the dark chocolate chips in a heatproof
bowl. Pour the simmering cream mixture over the
chocolate chips and whisk until melted and smooth.

Spoon about ½ cup of the ganache on top of the cake
batter all around the pan, being careful to not let
any ganache touch the edges of the pan. Bake until
a cake tester inserted into the center of the cake
comes out clean (it may have a trace of ganache),
35 to 38 minutes. Let cool completely in the pan
on a wire rack.

Turn the cake out of the Bundt pan, place on a
plate, and pour the remaining ganache over the
top. Sprinkle with mini chocolate chips and serve.

CAPPUCCINO STREUSEL CAKE

This cake is flavored strongly with coffee, as is the frosting on top, resulting in the perfect cake to eat with, well, coffee.

For the cake: In a small saucepan, heat the buttermilk, coffee, and vanilla over medium-low heat until the mixture is steaming but not simmering. Turn off the heat and let the coffee steep for 10 minutes. Strain the mixture through a fine-mesh strainer, and set aside to cool completely.

Preheat the oven to 375°F, and thoroughly grease and flour a 10-inch tube pan. In a bowl, mix together the flour, baking powder, salt, and cinnamon. In a large bowl, beat together the butter and granulated sugar until fluffy. Add the eggs and beat well. Add the flour mixture and the cooled coffee-buttermilk mixture in alternating additions, beating until smooth.

For the streusel: In a bowl, use a fork to mix together the brown sugar, flour, butter, and cinnamon until the mixture is crumbly.

Pour half the cake batter into the prepared pan and spread evenly. Sprinkle the streusel mixture evenly over the cake batter. Pour the remaining batter over the top, and smooth out to cover the streusel. Bake until a cake tester inserted into the center of the cake comes out clean, 35 to 40 minutes. Let cool completely in the pan on a wire rack before removing.

For the frosting: In a bowl, beat together the butter and powdered sugar until smooth. Add the coffee and espresso powder and beat well. Add the cream and beat until light and fluffy. Add a little more powdered sugar if needed. Spread over the cooled cake, and sprinkle with walnuts, if desired.

MAKES 8 TO 10 SERVINGS

FOR THE CAKE

1 cup buttermilk

3 tablespoons finely ground coffee

1 tablespoon vanilla extract

2¼ cups all-purpose flour

1½ teaspoons baking powder

½ teaspoon salt

½ teaspoon ground cinnamon

¾ cup plus 2 tablespoons unsalted butter, softened

1⅓ cups granulated sugar

3 eggs

FOR THE STREUSEL

⅓ cup firmly packed brown sugar

¼ cup all-purpose flour

3 tablespoons unsalted butter, chilled and cubed

1 teaspoon ground cinnamon

FOR THE FROSTING

1 cup unsalted butter, softened

1 cup powdered sugar, plus more as needed

¼ cup strongly brewed coffee, cooled

2 teaspoons espresso powder

1 tablespoon heavy cream

1 tablespoon chopped walnuts (optional)

PEACH UPSIDE-DOWN CAKE

Upside-down cakes are classic, but we're putting a twist on them in this recipe by using peaches instead of pineapples! You can use another stone fruit of your choice, or even more slices if you like.

MAKES 8 TO 10 SERVINGS

½ cup unsalted butter, softened

¾ cup granulated sugar

2 eggs

1 egg white

1 teaspoon vanilla extract

¼ cup whole milk

1½ cups plus 2 tablespoons cake flour

1½ teaspoons baking powder

1 teaspoon salt

⅓ cup unsalted butter, melted

¾ cup firmly packed dark brown sugar

2 firm but ripe peaches, pitted and sliced

Preheat the oven to 350°F, and grease and flour an 8-inch round cake pan. Line the bottom of the cake pan with parchment paper cut to fit. In a large bowl, beat together the butter and granulated sugar until fluffy. Beat in the whole eggs, egg white, and vanilla, and beat for 2 to 3 minutes. Mix in the milk. Add the flour, baking powder, and salt, and beat until combined.

Pour the melted butter into the bottom of the greased cake pan and tilt the pan around so the butter evenly coats the bottom. Sprinkle the brown sugar evenly over the butter. Arrange the peach slices on the bottom of the pan, on top of the butter and brown sugar, in one even layer. Pour the cake batter over the peaches, and spread evenly in the pan.

Bake until a cake tester inserted into the center of the cake comes out clean, 35 to 40 minutes. Let cool for 10 minutes.

Place a serving platter upside down on top of the pan. Using oven mitts, invert the platter and pan together in one swift motion. Give it a gentle shake, if needed, until the cake releases onto the platter. Cut into wedges to serve.

PISTACHIO-OLIVE OIL CAKE

It may sound a bit odd to make a cake that is heavily flavored with olive oil, but it's actually super awesome. The fruitiness of the oil comes through strongly, and the addition of pistachios pulls it together. All in all, it's something you may not have tried, but you definitely should!

MAKES 8 TO 10 SERVINGS

FOR THE CAKE

2¼ cups cake flour

¼ cup all-purpose flour

1 teaspoon baking powder

1 teaspoon salt

¾ cup olive oil

1½ cups granulated sugar

3 eggs

¾ cup whole milk

1 cup chopped pistachios

2 tablespoons coarse sugar
   (optional)

FOR THE ICING

¾ cup powdered sugar

2 to 3 tablespoons water

½ teaspoon vanilla extract

For the cake: Preheat the oven to 375°F. Grease an 8-inch round cake pan and line the bottom with parchment paper cut to fit. In a bowl, whisk together the cake flour, all-purpose flour, baking powder, and salt. In a large bowl, beat together the olive oil and granulated sugar until smooth. Beat in the eggs until combined. Add the flour mixture and milk in alternating additions, starting and ending with the flour mixture, beat until smooth between additions. Fold in the chopped pistachios. Pour the batter into the prepared pan, and evenly sprinkle the coarse sugar over the top, if desired. Bake until the top is dark golden and a cake tester inserted into the center of the cake comes out clean, 55 to 60 minutes. Let cool completely in the pan on a wire rack before removing.

For the icing: In a small bowl, stir together the powdered sugar, 2 tablespoons water, and the vanilla until smooth, adding more water for a thinner consistency. Drizzle the icing over the top of your cake. Cut into wedges to serve.

PLUM-ORANGE CAKE

Honestly, I don't like much fruit at all. But this cake, you guys, it's one of the best things I've ever made, and you gotta try it even if you're not much of a fruit lover, like me. Juicy plum slices top an orange-flavored pound cake that is dense, and sweet, and perfect.

MAKES 8 TO 10 SERVINGS

FOR THE CAKE

1½ cups cake flour

1 teaspoon salt

½ teaspoon baking powder

Finely grated zest of 1 orange

½ cup unsalted butter, softened

1 cup granulated sugar

2 eggs

1 teaspoon vanilla extract

1 teaspoon orange extract (optional)

¼ cup orange juice

2 ripe plums, pitted and thinly sliced

2 tablespoons coarse sugar

FOR THE ICING

1½ cups powdered sugar

2 to 3 tablespoons orange juice

For the cake: Preheat the oven to 350°F, and grease and flour a 9-by-5-inch loaf pan. In a bowl, whisk together the cake flour, salt, baking powder, and orange zest. In a large bowl, beat together the butter and granulated sugar until combined. Mix in the eggs, vanilla, and orange extract, if using. Add the flour mixture alternating with the orange juice, beginning and ending with the flour mixture. Mix the batter 1 to 2 minutes, until it has reached a very smooth consistency. Pour the batter into your prepared loaf pan, and spread evenly. Arrange the plum slices over the top of the batter. Sprinkle the coarse sugar evenly over the top.

Bake until a cake tester inserted into the center of the cake comes out clean, 50 to 55 minutes. Let cool completely before removing from the pan.

For the icing: In a bowl, whisk together the powdered sugar and 2 tablespoons orange juice, adding more juice as needed to reach a drizzly consistency.

Run a knife around the edges of your pan, and turn the cake out onto a plate. Drizzle icing over the cake liberally. Cut the finished cake into slices to serve.

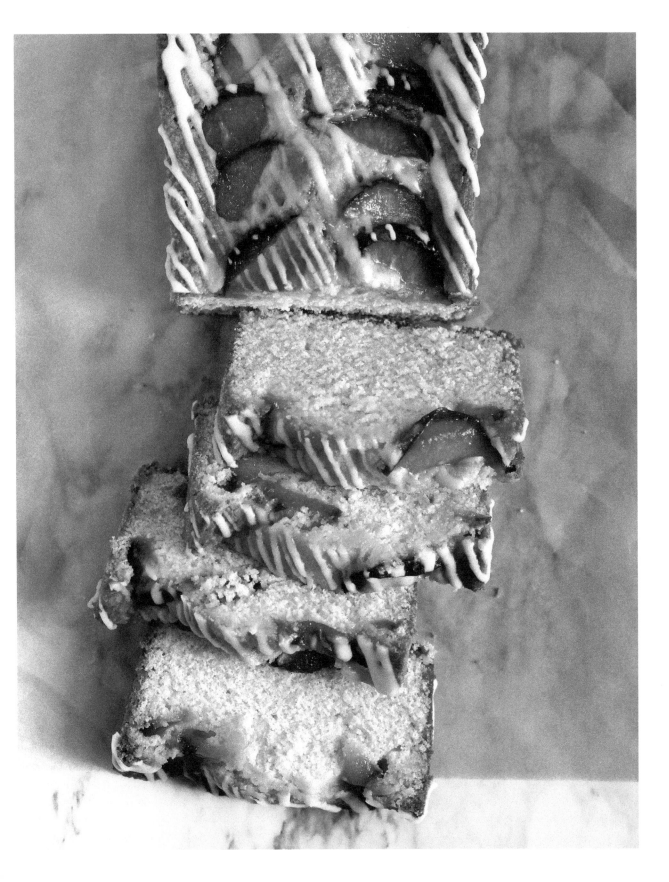

GINGERBREAD

This bread just screams the holidays to me. You might be more
familiar with gingerbread cookies than a classic gingerbread loaf,
but I promise this is Christmas morning in a pan. Cozy, spicy,
and moist. It'll be a new tradition in your house.

MAKES 8 TO 10 SERVINGS

For the gingerbread: Preheat the oven to 350°F, and
grease and flour a 9-by-5-inch loaf pan. In a bowl,
whisk together the flour, ginger, cinnamon, baking
soda, salt, cloves, and allspice. In a large bowl, beat
together the butter and brown sugar until fluffy.
Add the molasses, egg, and vanilla, and stir until
combined. Stir in the milk. Slowly add the flour
mixture and beat until completely incorporated.
Pour into the prepared pan and spread evenly.

Bake until a cake tester inserted into the center
comes out clean, 55 to 60 minutes. Cool in the pan
for 10 to 15 minutes.

For the icing: In a small bowl, whisk together the
powdered sugar, 2 tablespoons water, and vanilla
extract. Add more water as needed until you reach
your desired consistency. I like mine to be fairly thick.

Run a knife around the edges of your pan, and turn
the gingerbread out onto a plate. Drizzle your icing
over the top. Cut the finished gingerbread into slices
to serve.

FOR THE GINGERBREAD

2⅔ cups all-purpose flour

1½ teaspoons ground ginger

1½ teaspoons ground cinnamon

¾ teaspoon baking soda

½ teaspoon salt

¼ teaspoon ground cloves

¼ teaspoon ground allspice

½ cup unsalted butter, softened

½ cup firmly packed brown sugar

¾ cup molasses

1 egg

2 teaspoons vanilla extract

¼ cup whole milk

FOR THE ICING

1½ cups powdered sugar

2 to 3 tablespoons water

½ teaspoon vanilla extract

CLASSIC VANILLA CUPCAKES

Vanilla is my favorite cake—sorry to disappoint all you complex-flavor lovers. Here's a great classic vanilla cake in cupcake form, paired with an equally classic chocolate frosting. This is also a great base recipe that you can work other flavors into if you're feelin' experimental.

MAKES 12 CUPCAKES

FOR THE CUPCAKES

½ cup unsalted butter, softened

½ cup granulated sugar

2 eggs

¼ cup sour cream

1 teaspoon vanilla extract

¾ cup self-rising flour

¼ cup cake flour

½ teaspoon salt

2 tablespoons whole milk

FOR THE FROSTING

1 cup unsalted butter, softened

2 cups powdered sugar

3 tablespoons cocoa powder

¼ cup chopped dark chocolate, melted and cooled (see page 16)

3 tablespoons heavy cream

For the cupcakes: Preheat the oven to 350°F, and line 12 muffin cups with paper liners. In a large bowl, beat the butter and granulated sugar together until fluffy. Add the eggs, sour cream, and vanilla. The mixture will be slightly lumpy. Add the self-rising flour, cake flour, and salt. Mix until combined; it will be a thick batter. Mix in the milk until combined. Scoop the batter evenly into the prepared muffin cups. Bake until a cake tester inserted into the center of a cupcake comes out clean, 16 to 18 minutes. Let cool completely in the pan on a wire rack before frosting.

For the frosting: Beat together the butter, powdered sugar, and cocoa powder until thick and smooth. Beat in the melted and cooled chocolate and mix until combined. Add the cream and beat until fluffy. Frost the cupcakes any way you like, but make sure you do it liberally! I like to put the frosting in a piping bag fitted with a star tip and make pretty (but easy!) designs on top.

WHITE CUPCAKES

It's well known around these parts that I am a vanilla girl. Not, like, in general, but in cake. What can I say? Sometimes things are simple, you guys! These cupcakes are light white cake, topped with a fluffy Italian buttercream, and I promise they're everything vanilla cupcakes should be.

For the cupcakes: Preheat the oven to 350°F, and line 12 muffin cups with paper liners. In a large bowl, beat together the butter and sugar until light and fluffy. Add the egg whites and vanilla, and beat until smooth, 1 to 2 minutes. In a bowl, whisk together the cake flour, baking powder, and salt. Then, stir the flour mixture into the butter mixture until combined. Add the sour cream and heavy cream, and beat until smooth and thick. Evenly scoop the batter into the prepared muffin cups, and bake until a cake tester inserted into the center of a cupcake comes out clean, 18 to 20 minutes. Let cool completely in the pan on a wire rack.

For the frosting: In a large heatproof bowl, whisk the egg whites until soft peaks form. Meanwhile, in a small saucepan, stir together the sugar, water, and corn syrup. Heat the sugar mixture until it reaches 230°F on an instant-read thermometer. With your mixer on, carefully pour the hot sugar mixture into the egg whites in a very slow stream, until it has been completely incorporated. Beat the mixture until it has completely cooled, and stiff, glossy peaks have formed, about 10 minutes. Mix in the softened butter, 1 tablespoon at a time, until all of the butter has been added. Continue beating until the mixture comes together and becomes smooth and fluffy. Add the vanilla and salt and beat to combine. Frost the cupcakes any way you like. I like to pipe on the frosting in a wide swirl using a plain pastry tip, then decorate with white sprinkles.

MAKES 12 CUPCAKES

FOR THE CUPCAKES
½ cup unsalted butter, softened

¾ cup sugar

3 egg whites

2 teaspoons vanilla extract

1½ cups cake flour

1½ teaspoons baking powder

½ teaspoon salt

¼ cup sour cream

2 tablespoons heavy cream

FOR THE FROSTING
3 egg whites

1 cup sugar

⅓ cup water

1 tablespoon light corn syrup

1¼ cups unsalted butter, softened

2 teaspoons vanilla extract

¼ teaspoon salt

White sprinkles for garnish (optional)

CHOCOLATE CUPCAKES

Here's another great classic, made with deep, fudgy flavors.
I made these with my little nephew, and he chose the
colorful sprinkles on top, which I highly recommend.

MAKES 12 CUPCAKES

FOR THE CUPCAKES

¼ cup boiling water

¼ cup dark cocoa powder

½ cup unsalted butter, softened

½ cup granulated sugar

2 eggs

¼ cup sour cream

2 tablespoons whole milk

1 teaspoon vanilla extract

1 cup all-purpose flour

1½ teaspoons baking powder

½ teaspoon salt

FOR THE FROSTING

¾ cup unsalted butter, softened

1½ cups powdered sugar,
  plus more if needed

2 tablespoons dark cocoa powder

⅓ cup chopped milk chocolate,
  melted and cooled (see page 16)

¼ cup heavy cream, plus more
  if needed

Pinch of salt

Sprinkles for garnish (optional)

For the cupcakes: Preheat the oven to 350°F, and line 12 muffin cups with paper liners. In a small bowl, mix together the boiling water and cocoa powder until smooth. Set aside. In a bowl, beat together the softened butter and granulated sugar until fluffy. Add the eggs, sour cream, milk, and vanilla, and mix until combined. Mix in the flour, baking powder, and salt. Beat until smooth and well blended, 1 to 2 minutes. Mix in the cocoa powder mixture until completely incorporated. Divide the batter evenly between the prepared muffin cups. Bake until a cake tester inserted into the center of a cupcake comes out clean, 15 to 18 minutes. Let cool completely in the pan on a wire rack before frosting.

For the frosting: In a bowl, beat together the butter, powdered sugar, and cocoa powder until mixed. Add the melted chocolate, cream, and salt. Beat until the frosting is light and fluffy. Add more heavy cream, 1 tablespoon at a time, if the frosting is too thick, and more powdered sugar, ¼ cup at a time, if it is too thin. Pile the frosting on top of the cupcakes and top with sprinkles, if using.

CHOCOLATE-WHISKEY CUPCAKES

These cupcakes offer everything you want in a chocolate cupcake after a hard day's work: a sweet, dark-chocolate cupcake that has the bitter, woodsy flavors of whiskey. Don't automatically reach for the bottom shelf at the liquor store—choose a whiskey you like to drink because baking is going to bring out its flavors!

For the cupcakes: Preheat the oven to 375°F, and line 24 muffin cups with paper liners. In a bowl, whisk together the cake flour, cocoa powder, baking soda, baking powder, and salt. In another bowl, stir together the buttermilk, coffee, and whiskey. In a large bowl, beat together the granulated sugar, brown sugar, and oil until blended. Beat in the eggs. Add the flour mixture and coffee mixture to the oil mixture, beginning and ending with the flour mixture and beating well between additions. Beat until the ingredients are completely combined. Divide the batter between the prepared muffin cups, filling each cup about three-quarters full. Bake until a cake tester inserted into the center of a cupcake comes out clean, 18 to 20 minutes. Let cool completely in the pan on a wire rack before frosting.

For the frosting: In a bowl, beat together the butter, powdered sugar, and cocoa powder until well blended and smooth. Add the cream, whiskey, vanilla, and salt, and beat until the frosting is fluffy and smooth, several minutes more. There's no need to be fancy when frosting these. Just pile it right on, sprinkle with coarse sugar, if you like a little extra texture, and indulge!

MAKES 24 CUPCAKES

FOR THE CUPCAKES

2½ cups cake flour

¾ cup dark cocoa powder

1½ teaspoons baking soda

1 teaspoon baking powder

1 teaspoon salt

¾ cup buttermilk

½ cup strongly brewed coffee, cooled

½ cup whiskey (I use bourbon, but you can use rye if you prefer)

1½ cups granulated sugar

½ cup firmly packed brown sugar

½ cup vegetable oil

2 eggs

FOR THE FROSTING

2 cups unsalted butter, softened

5 cups powdered sugar

¼ cup dark cocoa powder

¼ cup heavy cream

3 tablespoons whiskey

½ teaspoon vanilla extract

½ teaspoon salt

Coarse sugar for garnish (optional)

TRIPLE-LEMON CUPCAKES

These lemon cupcakes are filled with a sweet lemon mousse that you'll want to eat with a spoon or use to top pancakes. The cake is also lightly lemon flavored, and the frosting ties it all together!

MAKES 12 CUPCAKES

FOR THE CUPCAKES

½ cup unsalted butter, softened

¾ cup granulated sugar

2 eggs

2 tablespoons sour cream

2 teaspoons lemon extract

2 teaspoons finely grated lemon zest

1½ cups cake flour

1½ teaspoons baking powder

¼ teaspoon salt

¼ cup whole milk

FOR THE FILLING

1 cup heavy cream

¼ cup purchased lemon curd

FOR THE FROSTING

¾ cup unsalted butter, softened

2 cups powdered sugar

¼ cup purchased lemon curd

1 tablespoon lemon juice

1 teaspoon finely grated lemon zest

¼ cup heavy cream

White or yellow sprinkles for garnish (optional)

For the cupcakes: Preheat the oven to 350°F, and line 12 muffin cups with paper liners. In a bowl, beat together the butter and granulated sugar until fluffy. Add the eggs, sour cream, lemon extract, and zest. Mix until combined. Beat in the flour, baking powder, and salt. Mix for several minutes, until completely combined. Add the milk and mix to combine. Scoop the batter evenly into the prepared muffin cups. Bake until a cake tester inserted into the center of a cupcake comes out clean, 15 to 18 minutes. Let cool completely in the pan on a wire rack before filling and frosting.

For the filling: In a bowl, whip the cream until stiff peaks form. Fold in the lemon curd.

For the frosting: In a bowl, beat together the butter and powdered sugar until smooth. Mix in the lemon curd, lemon juice, and zest. Beat in the cream until the mixture becomes light and fluffy.

To assemble, use a sharp knife to remove a ½- to 1-inch round section from the center of each cupcake (save these for snacking!). Spoon the filling into the cupcake centers, filling the holes. Top the filling with frosting—I like to put the frosting in a piping bag fitted with a large star tip and pipe a single rosette on top of each cupcake. Scatter with sprinkles, if you like, and serve.

SPICE CUPCAKES

Spice cake is just warmth and sweetness all wrapped up into a package—a cupcake-sized package, in this case. This version is topped with a marshmallowy brown sugar frosting that I'm obsessed with. If you've never made marshmallow frosting or filling at home, now is the time!

For the cupcakes: Preheat the oven to 350°F, and line 24 muffin cups with paper liners. In a large bowl, beat together the butter and granulated sugar until fluffy. Add the eggs, sour cream, and vanilla, and mix until combined. In another bowl, whisk together the cake flour, baking powder, cinnamon, nutmeg, allspice, salt, and ginger. Slowly add the flour mixture to the butter mixture until completely incorporated. The batter will be thick. Stir in the heavy cream. Scoop the batter evenly into the prepared muffin cups. Bake until a cake tester inserted into the center of a cupcake comes out clean, 18 to 20 minutes. Let cool completely in the pan on a wire rack before frosting.

For the frosting: Place the brown sugar, corn syrup, and water in a saucepan. Over medium-high heat, bring the mixture to a boil. Let the mixture boil, stirring occasionally, until it is dark brown in color and fairly thick, about 8 minutes. Meanwhile, in the bowl of a stand mixer, beat the egg whites and cream of tartar until soft peaks form. With the mixer running, carefully pour the hot sugar mixture into the egg whites in a slow, steady stream. Beat the mixture until it has cooled and thick, glossy peaks have formed, about 5 to 10 minutes. Beat in the vanilla and cinnamon until combined.

Frost the cupcakes as you like. Be sure to use a knife to give them a perky little peak in the center!

MAKES 24 CUPCAKES

FOR THE CUPCAKES

1 cup unsalted butter, softened

1½ cups granulated sugar

4 eggs

½ cup sour cream

1 teaspoon vanilla extract

2½ cups cake flour

3 teaspoons baking powder

1½ teaspoons ground cinnamon

½ teaspoon ground nutmeg

½ teaspoon ground allspice

½ teaspoon salt

¼ teaspoon ground ginger

¼ cup heavy cream

FOR THE FROSTING

1 cup firmly packed brown sugar

½ cup light corn syrup

2 tablespoons water

5 egg whites

½ teaspoon cream of tartar

1 teaspoon vanilla extract

1 teaspoon ground cinnamon

COCONUT CAKE

Wanna know a secret? Coconut ain't my thing, guys. That being said,
I ate more than one slice of this layered beauty—it's light, fluffy, and
has just enough coconut flavor to impress but not overwhelm. Plus, after
you clean the mess in your kitchen, it's pretty impressive looking!

**MAKES 8 TO 10 SERVINGS,
AS A 3-LAYER OR 2-LAYER CAKE**

FOR THE CAKE

1 cup unsalted butter, softened

1½ cups sugar

6 egg whites

½ cup sour cream

1 teaspoon vanilla extract

2½ cups cake flour

3 teaspoons baking powder

½ teaspoon salt

¼ cup coconut milk liquid (reserve
   the solids for the frosting)

¾ cup unsweetened coconut flakes

FOR THE SYRUP

½ cup coconut milk liquid

½ cup sugar

For the cake: Preheat the oven to 350°F, and grease
and flour three 6-inch or two 8-inch round cake
pans. In a large bowl, beat together the butter and
sugar until fluffy. Add the egg whites and beat for
several minutes. Add the sour cream and vanilla
and beat until smooth and incorporated. Mix in the
cake flour, baking powder, and salt until completely
incorporated. Beat in the coconut milk liquid until
the mixture is smooth. Fold in the coconut flakes.
Divide the batter evenly between your cake pans,
spreading the tops evenly. Bake the cakes until a cake
tester inserted into the centers comes out clean, about
30 minutes for 6-inch cakes or 35 minutes for 8-inch
cakes. Let cool completely in the pans on wire racks
before removing.

For the syrup: In a small saucepan, bring the coconut
milk liquid and sugar to a boil. Remove from the
heat and let cool completely.

When the cake layers and syrup have cooled, use a
serrated knife to trim off the tops of the layers to
make them flat. Brush the cooled syrup generously
on top of the cake layers. Reserve the remaining
syrup—it's great in coffee! Cover the soaked cake
layers with plastic wrap.

CONTINUED ON NEXT PAGE

COCONUT CAKE (CON'T)

FOR THE FROSTING AND TOPPING

1½ cups unsweetened coconut flakes

6 egg whites

1¼ cups sugar

1½ cups unsalted butter, softened

1 teaspoon vanilla extract

⅛ teaspoon salt

½ cup coconut milk solids, whipped

For the frosting and topping: In a dry frying pan over medium heat, toast the coconut flakes until lightly golden brown, stirring regularly to avoid burning. This should take 5 to 10 minutes. In the top part of a double boiler, whisk together the egg whites and sugar. Warm over simmering water until the mixture reaches 160°F on an instant-read thermometer, or until the sugar has dissolved completely. Transfer the mixture to the bowl of a stand mixer fitted with the whisk attachment, or pour into a heatproof bowl and use a hand mixer. Whisk the mixture on medium-high speed until it is completely cool and stiff peaks have formed, about 10 minutes. Beat in the butter, 1 tablespoon at a time, until fully incorporated. The mixture may look thin, and it might separate, but just keep beating—I promise, it will come together. Continue to beat until the mixture becomes light and fluffy, another 10 minutes. Beat in the vanilla and salt until combined. Add in the whipped coconut milk solids, and continue to beat until fully mixed and fluffy.

To assemble a 3-layer cake, spread ⅓ cup of the frosting in a thin, even layer on a cake layer. Place a second cake layer on top of the filled first layer, lining up the edges. Repeat the filling steps as for the first layer. Top with the last layer, lining up the edges.

For a 2-layer cake, follow the instructions for a 3-layer cake, using ½ cup of the filling between the layers.

When the layers are assembled, frost your cake as desired, and use the toasted coconut to garnish. I like to press the toasted coconut into the frosting all around the sides of the cake and leave the top naked.

RED VELVET SHEET-BAKED LAYER CAKE

This is a cake to make for a crowd—it's huge. And it's also a little messy, but that's just what you get with the best-tasting, lightest-and-fluffiest cream cheese frosting around. It's everything you want in a red velvet cake.

For the cake: Preheat the oven to 350°F. Grease a 12-by-16-inch rimmed baking sheet, and lay a piece of parchment paper on the bottom of the pan, greasing the top of the parchment as well. In a bowl, whisk together the cake flour, cocoa powder, baking soda, and salt. In another large bowl, beat together the butter, oil, and sugar until thoroughly combined. Beat in the eggs, vanilla, and vinegar. Add the flour mixture and buttermilk in alternating additions, starting and ending with the flour mixture, beating each addition until completely incorporated before adding the next. After the last addition, beat until the batter is smooth and thoroughly combined, an additional 1 to 2 minutes. Add the red food coloring, and beat on a low speed until it is fully incorporated and there are no uncolored bits of batter.

Spread the batter evenly in the prepared pan, using a small offset spatula to get it into all the corners. Bake until a cake tester inserted into the center of the cake comes out clean, about 25 minutes. Let cool for 15 to 20 minutes in the pan, then flip the cake onto a cutting board, peel off the parchment paper, and let cool completely.

CONTINUED ON NEXT PAGE

MAKES 16 TO 18 SERVINGS

FOR THE CAKE

3½ cups cake flour

3 tablespoons dark cocoa powder

1 teaspoon baking soda

1 teaspoon salt

1 cup unsalted butter, softened

½ cup vegetable oil

2 cups sugar

4 eggs

2 teaspoons vanilla extract

1 teaspoon white vinegar

1 cup buttermilk

2½ tablespoons red food coloring

RED VELVET SHEET-BAKED LAYER CAKE
(CON'T)

Using a serrated knife, trim the edges of the cake so that you have clean, sharp edges. Take the trimmings, and crumble them roughly. Place the crumbs on a baking sheet and toast in a 350°F oven until the crumbs start to brown on the edges, about 10 minutes. Cool the crumbs, then crush them finely.

For the frosting: In a bowl, beat together the cream cheese, butter, and vanilla until smooth. Slowly beat in the powdered sugar and salt until completely incorporated. Add the heavy cream and mix for several minutes, until the frosting has become slightly fluffy.

To assemble, cut the cooled and trimmed cake into three even sections. Place the first layer onto a platter, and cover with about a quarter of the frosting, creating an even layer. Repeat with the second and third layers, frosting the sides of the cake last. Sprinkle the cake crumbs onto the top of the cake, completely coating it, and press them gently into the frosting. Cut into slices to serve.

FOR THE FROSTING

- 2 packages (8 ounces *each*) cream cheese, softened
- ½ cup unsalted butter, softened
- 2 teaspoons vanilla extract
- 5 cups powdered sugar
- ⅛ teaspoon salt
- 2 tablespoons heavy cream

STRAWBERRIES & CREAM CAKE

Strawberries and cream are too much of a classic to skip. But you can swap out the strawberry preserves that flavor the cake for any other preserves you prefer—blackberry, peach, even orange marmalade. Get fancy with it, guys!

MAKES 8 TO 10 SERVINGS, AS A 3-LAYER OR 2-LAYER CAKE

FOR THE FILLING

1¼ teaspoons powdered unflavored gelatin

1 tablespoon cold water

3 egg yolks

¼ cup granulated sugar

⅓ cup heavy cream

¾ cup whole milk

1 teaspoon vanilla extract

FOR THE CAKE

1 cup unsalted butter, softened

1¼ cups granulated sugar

4 eggs

½ cup sour cream

2 teaspoons vanilla extract

2 cups cake flour

3 teaspoons baking powder

½ teaspoon salt

¼ cup heavy cream

For the filling: In a small dish, mix together the gelatin and cold water. Set aside. In a small heatproof bowl, whisk together the egg yolks and granulated sugar until thick and pale. In a saucepan over medium heat, combine the cream, milk, and vanilla. Heat until boiling. Whisking continuously, pour about 1 cup of the hot liquid into the egg yolk mixture. Then, pour the egg yolk mixture back into the saucepan with the remaining hot milk, and continue to cook, stirring frequently, until the mixture is thick. Remove from the heat, then whisk in the gelatin mixture, continuing to whisk until it is completely incorporated. Pour the mixture into a glass bowl, and cover with plastic wrap. Refrigerate until it is completely chilled.

For the cake: Preheat the oven to 350°F, and grease and flour three 6-inch or two 8-inch round cake pans. In a large bowl, beat together the butter and sugar until fluffy. Add the eggs, sour cream, and vanilla. Add the cake flour, baking powder, and salt, and mix until combined. Pour in the heavy cream and continue to mix until smooth. Divide the batter evenly between the prepared pans, spreading the tops evenly. Bake the cakes until a cake tester inserted into the centers comes out clean, 30 to 35 minutes for 6-inch cakes, and 35 to 40 minutes for 8-inch cakes. Let cool completely in the pans on wire racks before removing.

CONTINUED ON NEXT PAGE

STRAWBERRIES & CREAM CAKE
(CON'T)

FOR THE FROSTING

2 cups unsalted butter, softened

4 cups powdered sugar

¾ cup strawberry preserves

⅛ teaspoon salt

¼ cup heavy cream

Red food coloring, if desired

White sprinkles for garnish (optional)

For the frosting: In a bowl, beat together the butter and powdered sugar until smooth. Add ½ cup of the strawberry preserves and the salt, and beat until smooth. Add the heavy cream, and beat until the mixture becomes light and fluffy. If desired, add a few drops of red food coloring to adjust the color of the frosting to your liking. Put the frosting in a piping bag with a plain tip.

To assemble, use a serrated knife to trim each cake layer so that it is flat. For a 3-layer cake, spread 2 tablespoons strawberry preserves in a thin, even layer on a cake layer. Then pipe a small ring of the pink frosting around the edges of the layer. Use a small offset spatula to spread the center with about ¼ to ⅓ cup of the cream filling. Place a second cake layer on top of the filled first layer, lining up the edges. Repeat the filling steps as for the first layer. Top with the last layer, lining up the edges.

For a 2-layer cake, follow the instructions for a 3-layer cake, using ¼ cup preserves and ⅓ to ½ cup of the filling.

When the layers are assembled, go ahead and frost and decorate the cake as desired. I like to pipe most of the frosting onto the top and sides of the cake, then use a cake spatula to smooth it all out to create a clean look. Sometimes I'll use a star pastry tip to pipe some fancy rosettes and decorate with sprinkles too.

OMBRÉ CHOCOLATE CAKE

For those days when you need chocolate, here's the right cake. Or for those days when you need the right birthday treat, here's your cake. Or for no good reason at all, here's the cake you need to bake right now.

For the filling: Put the chopped chocolate in a heatproof bowl, and place a mesh strainer over the top. Set aside. In a small saucepan, heat the cream, vanilla, and salt over medium heat until boiling. While the cream mixture heats, place the egg yolks and sugar in a small bowl, and whisk together until pale and thick. Whisking continuously, pour half of the hot cream into the yolk mixture. Then pour the yolk mixture back into the pan with the remaining cream, and continue to cook until thick, stirring frequently, about 5 more minutes. Pour the thickened cream mixture through the strainer over the chocolate. Whisk the mixture until the chocolate is melted and the mixture is smooth. Cover the mixture by placing plastic wrap directly on top, and chill completely in the refrigerator.

For the cake: Preheat the oven to 375°F, and grease and flour three 6-inch round cake pans. In a bowl, whisk together the cake flour, cocoa powder, baking powder, and salt. In a large bowl, beat together the sugar and oil. Add the vanilla and eggs, and stir until blended. Add the flour mixture and buttermilk in alternating additions, starting and ending with the flour mixture and beating until incorporated before adding the next addition. Divide the batter between your prepared pans, spreading the tops evenly. Bake until a cake tester inserted into the centers comes out clean, 25 to 30 minutes. Let cool completely in the pans on wire racks before removing.

CONTINUED ON NEXT PAGE

MAKES 8 TO 10 SERVINGS, AS A 3-LAYER OR 2-LAYER CAKE

FOR THE FILLING

4 ounces dark chocolate, chopped

1 cup heavy cream

1 teaspoon vanilla extract

⅛ teaspoon salt

2 egg yolks

2 tablespoons sugar

FOR THE CAKE

2 cups cake flour

¾ cup dark cocoa powder

2 teaspoons baking powder

½ teaspoon salt

1½ cups sugar

⅔ cup vegetable oil

1 teaspoon vanilla extract

2 eggs

1 cup buttermilk

OMBRÉ CHOCOLATE CAKE (CON'T)

For the frosting: In the top part of a double boiler, whisk together the egg whites and sugar. Warm over simmering water until the mixture reaches 160°F on an instant-read thermometer, or until the sugar has completely dissolved. Transfer the mixture to the bowl of a stand mixer fitted with the whisk attachment, or pour into a heatproof bowl and use a hand mixer. Beat the mixture until it is completely cool and stiff peaks have formed, about 10 minutes. Add the butter 1 tablespoon at a time until fully incorporated. The mixture will look thin and may even begin to separate. Continue to beat until it becomes thick and fluffy, another 5 to 10 minutes. Beat in the vanilla and salt.

Add half of the melted chocolate to the frosting, and whip until completely incorporated. Set aside about one-third of the mixture in another bowl. Add the remaining melted chocolate to the frosting and beat until incorporated. Set aside half of this new mixture in a third bowl. Then sift in the cocoa powder into the remaining frosting mixture and mix until incorporated. Now you have 3 shades of chocolate frosting.

To assemble, use a serrated knife to trim each cake layer so that it is flat. Spread half of the filling evenly on one layer. Place the second layer on top, lining up the edges. Spread the remaining filling over the second layer. Top with the third layer, lining up the edges.

Put each shade of frosting into a different resealable plastic zipper bag, and cut a hole in the corner. Then, starting with the darkest shade, pipe the frosting onto the bottom third of the cake all around the circumference. Repeat with the remaining shades. Use a cake spatula to smooth out the frosting on the sides and top to blend together!

FOR THE FROSTING

5 egg whites

1¼ cups sugar

1¼ cups unsalted butter, softened

1 teaspoon vanilla extract

⅛ teaspoon salt

4 ounces dark chocolate, chopped, melted and cooled (see page 16)

2 tablespoons dark cocoa powder, sifted (optional)

VANILLA LAYER CAKE

This cake is everything vanilla, in the best way possible. The cream filling
is super smooth and tasty, and the frosting is a Swiss meringue,
which is basically like putting vanilla clouds all over your cake!

**MAKES 8 TO 10 SERVINGS,
AS A 3-LAYER OR 2-LAYER CAKE**

FOR THE CAKE

2½ cups cake flour

3 teaspoons baking powder

1 teaspoon salt

6 egg whites

½ teaspoon cream of tartar

½ cup vegetable oil

1¾ cups sugar

2 teaspoons vanilla extract

1 teaspoon almond extract

1¼ cups whole milk

FOR THE FILLING

1¼ teaspoons powdered unflavored
    gelatin

1 tablespoon cold water

3 egg yolks

¼ cup sugar

⅓ cup heavy cream

¾ cup whole milk

1 teaspoon vanilla extract

For the cake: Preheat the oven to 350°F, and grease
and flour three 6-inch or two 8-inch round cake pans.
In a bowl, whisk together the cake flour, baking
powder, and salt. In a large bowl, beat the egg whites
and cream of tartar until stiff peaks form. In another
large bowl, beat together the oil, sugar, vanilla, and
almond extract. Add the flour mixture and the milk
in alternating additions, beginning and ending with
the flour mixture, and mixing until smooth before
adding the next addition. Divide the batter between
your prepared cake pans, spreading the tops evenly.
Bake the cakes until a cake tester inserted into the
centers comes out clean, about 25 minutes for 6-inch
cakes and 30 minutes for 8-inch cakes. Cool the cakes
completely in the pans on wire racks before removing.

For the filling: In a small dish, mix together the
gelatin and cold water. Set aside. In a small heatproof
bowl, whisk together the egg yolks and sugar
until thick and pale. In a saucepan over medium
heat, combine the cream, milk, and vanilla. Heat
until boiling. Whisking continuously, pour about
1 cup of the hot liquid into the egg yolk mixture.
Then pour the egg yolk mixture back into the
saucepan with the remaining hot milk, and continue
to cook, stirring frequently, until the mixture is
thick. Remove from the heat, then whisk the gelatin
mixture in, continuing to whisk until it is completely

CONTINUED ON NEXT PAGE

VANILLA LAYER CAKE (CON'T)

FOR THE FROSTING

5 egg whites

1¼ cups sugar

1¼ cups unsalted butter, softened

2 teaspoons vanilla extract

⅛ teaspoon salt

Edible golden sugar pearls
for garnish (optional)

incorporated. Pour the mixture into a glass bowl, and cover with plastic wrap. Refrigerate until it is completely chilled.

For the frosting: In the top part of a double boiler, whisk together the egg whites and sugar. Warm over simmering water until the mixture reaches 160°F on an instant-read thermometer, or until the sugar has completely dissolved. Transfer the mixture to the bowl of a stand mixer fitted with the whisk attachment, or pour into a heatproof bowl and use a hand mixer. Beat the mixture until it is completely cool and stiff peaks have formed, about 10 minutes. Add the butter, 1 tablespoon at a time, until fully incorporated. The mixture will look thin and may even begin to separate. Continue to beat until it becomes thick and fluffy, another 5 to 10 minutes. Beat in the vanilla and salt.

To assemble, use a serrated knife to trim each cake layer so that it is flat. Spread half of the filling evenly on one layer. Place the second layer on top, lining up the edges. Spread the remaining filling over the second layer. Top with the third layer, lining up the edges. Frost as desired.

For a 2-layer cake, follow the instructions for a 3-layer cake, using ¼ to ⅓ cup of the filling.

Frost the cake in any design that you like. I like to apply the frosting with a cake spatula, creating a really clean, smooth surface, then using a tool called a "cake comb" or even a fork to make straight lines all around. On days I'm feeling dramatic, I'll top the cake with sugar pearls!

WHITE CHOCOLATE–RASPBERRY CAKE

This cake is kind of a stunner. White chocolate and raspberry has always been a flavor combination that screams fancy to me, and this cake is no exception. Layers of raspberry cake, raspberry jam, and white chocolate frosting make this a dramatic beauty, but it's far easier to make than you might think.

For the cake: Preheat the oven to 350°F, and grease and flour three 6-inch or two 8-inch round cake pans. In a bowl, whisk together the cake flour, baking powder, and salt. In a large bowl, beat together the butter and sugar until fluffy. Mix in the egg whites, whole egg, sour cream, raspberry preserves, and vanilla until combined. Add the flour mixture and the milk in alternating additions, starting and ending with the flour mixture and mixing until well blended before adding the next addition. In a small bowl, toss the fresh raspberries with the all-purpose flour, then fold into the cake batter until evenly distributed. Divide the batter between your prepared pans, spreading the tops evenly. Bake until a cake tester inserted into the centers comes out clean, 35 to 40 minutes for 6-inch cakes, or 45 to 50 minutes for 8-inch cakes. Cool the cakes completely in the pans on wire racks before removing.

For the frosting: In the top part of a double boiler, whisk together the egg whites and sugar. Warm over simmering water until the mixture reaches 160°F on an instant-read thermometer, or until the sugar has completely dissolved. Transfer the mixture to the bowl of a stand mixer fitted with the whisk attachment, or pour into a heatproof bowl and use a hand mixer. Beat the mixture until it is completely cool and stiff peaks have formed, about 10 minutes.

MAKES 8 TO 10 SERVINGS, AS A 3-LAYER OR 2-LAYER CAKE

FOR THE CAKE

3½ cups cake flour

1½ teaspoons baking powder

½ teaspoon salt

1 cup unsalted butter, softened

1½ cups sugar

3 egg whites

1 whole egg

½ cup sour cream

2 tablespoons raspberry preserves

1 teaspoon vanilla extract

¾ cup whole milk

2 cups fresh raspberries

1 tablespoon all-purpose flour

FOR THE FROSTING

5 egg whites

1¼ cups sugar

1¾ cups unsalted butter, softened

1 teaspoon vanilla extract

¼ teaspoon salt

4 ounces white chocolate, melted (see page 16)

CONTINUED ON NEXT PAGE

WHITE CHOCOLATE-RASPBERRY CAKE
(CON'T)

Add the butter, 1 tablespoon at a time, until fully incorporated. The mixture will look thin and may even begin to separate. Continue to beat until it becomes thick and fluffy frosting, another 5 to 10 minutes. Beat in the vanilla, salt, and melted white chocolate.

For the ganache: Pour the heavy cream into a large heatproof bowl. Heat in the microwave on high in short bursts until boiling. Whisk in the white chocolate chips until the mixture is smooth. Set aside to cool. When you are ready to use, you want the mixture to be lukewarm and pourable.

To assemble, use a serrated knife to trim each cake layer so that it is flat. For a 3-layer cake, spread half of the raspberry preserves on a cake layer. Using a cake spatula, carefully spread a thin layer of frosting over the preserves. Place a second cake layer on top of the filled first layer, lining up the edges. Repeat the filling steps for the first layer. Top with the last layer, lining up the edges.

For a 2-layer cake, follow the instructions for a 3-layer cake, using all the preserves and a medium-thin layer of frosting between the layers.

Using a cake spatula, apply the remaining frosting to the top and sides of the cake, smoothing it evenly. I like to leave some texture on the sides for a little flair. Then, using a plastic bag or piping bag with a thin tip, pipe the ganache around the edges of the top of the cake, allowing it to drip off in several areas. Cover the top of the cake with more ganache in an even layer. Decorate as desired. My favorite way is to save a little frosting and pipe it in rosettes using a star tip, then top each rosette with a fresh raspberry.

FOR THE GANACHE
½ cup heavy cream
1 cup white chocolate chips

½ cup raspberry preserves
Fresh raspberries for garnish (optional)

VANILLA LATTE CAKE

Vanilla and coffee just go together, if you ask me. Vanilla is the perfect flavor to cut through the bitterness of coffee, and cake is the perfect format to bring them together! Okay, lattes are great too, but this cake, you guys . . . really.

MAKES 10 TO 12 SERVINGS

FOR THE CAKE

1 cup egg whites (from about 8 eggs)

½ teaspoon cream of tartar

2 cups granulated sugar

4½ cups cake flour, sifted

2½ teaspoons baking powder

2 teaspoons salt

1 cup whole milk

1 cup water

⅔ cup vegetable oil

2 teaspoons vanilla extract
   or vanilla bean paste

FOR THE BUTTERCREAM

3 cups unsalted butter, softened

6 cups powdered sugar

⅓ cup espresso powder

1 teaspoon vanilla extract

⅓ cup heavy cream

White sprinkles for garnish (optional)

For the cake: Preheat the oven to 375°F, and grease and flour four 8-inch round cake pans. (You can also bake in batches, like I do, and prepare 2 pans at a time.) In a bowl, whip the egg whites and cream of tartar until stiff peaks form. Slowly add the granulated sugar into the egg whites and beat until they are stiff and silky. In a large bowl, sift together the cake flour, baking powder, and salt. Add the milk, water, oil, and vanilla, and beat with an electric mixer for 2 minutes. Gently fold the egg whites into the flour mixture until fully combined. Divide the batter between the prepared cake pans, spreading the tops evenly. Bake until a cake tester inserted into the centers comes out clean, 25 to 27 minutes. Let cool completely in the pans on wire racks before removing.

For the buttercream: In a large bowl, beat together the butter and powdered sugar until smooth. Add the espresso powder and vanilla. Then beat in the cream until the frosting becomes fluffy.

To assemble, use a serrated knife to trim each cake layer so that it is flat. Evenly spread ½ cup of the buttercream on a cake layer. Place a second cake layer on top, lining up the edges. Repeat the filling steps as for the first layer. Top with the last layer, lining up the edges.

Frost the top and the sides of the cake with the remaining buttercream, using a cake spatula when applying the buttercream to create a clean, smooth surface. Decorate with sprinkles, if desired.

DOUBLE-CHOCOLATE WHOOPIE PIES

Whoopie pies are actually cake sandwiches and, with their moist, dark-chocolate shells enclosing fluffy buttery filling, they pretty much scream happiness. These ones are super chocolatey, and easy, and everything in between.

For the cakes: Preheat the oven to 350°F, and line a baking sheet with parchment paper or a nonstick mat. In a heatproof bowl, mix together the boiling water and cocoa powder until smooth. Set aside. In a large bowl, beat together the butter and granulated sugar until fluffy. Stir in the eggs and sour cream. Add the flour, baking powder, and salt. Beat until combined. Beat in the cocoa mixture, and mix until it is completely combined.

Scoop approximately 2 tablespoons of batter onto your baking sheet at a time, leaving space for the cakes to spread while baking. Bake until a cake tester inserted into the center of a cake comes out clean, 10 to 12 minutes. Cool completely on a wire rack before filling.

For the filling: In a bowl, beat together the butter and powdered sugar until fluffy. Add the vanilla and salt. Mix in the cocoa powder until blended.

To assemble, spread some of the filling on the flat side of one cake, and then top it with another cake, pressing the cakes together lightly.

MAKES ABOUT 12 PIES

FOR THE CAKES

½ cup boiling water

½ cup dark cocoa powder

1 cup unsalted butter, softened

1 cup granulated sugar

2 eggs

½ cup sour cream

2 cups all-purpose flour

1 teaspoon baking powder

½ teaspoon salt

FOR THE FILLING

1 cup unsalted butter, softened

2 cups powdered sugar

½ teaspoon vanilla extract

¼ teaspoon salt

¼ cup dark cocoa powder

BLACKBERRY CHEESECAKE

A thick, chunky, and tart blackberry sauce tops this vanilla cheesecake, and it will not fail to impress, I promise. Cheesecake is one of those things that simply needs to be made sometimes, and maybe now is one of those times.

MAKES 10 TO 12 SERVINGS

FOR THE CRUST

15 graham crackers

⅓ cup sugar

5 tablespoons unsalted butter, melted

FOR THE FILLING

4 packages (8 ounces *each*) cream cheese, softened

1½ cups sugar

⅔ cup whole milk

4 eggs

2 teaspoons vanilla extract

1 cup sour cream

⅓ cup all-purpose flour, sifted

½ teaspoon salt

Finely grated zest of 1 lemon

FOR THE BLACKBERRY TOPPING

2 pints blackberries

¼ cup sugar

Juice of 1 lemon

1 tablespoon cornstarch

¼ teaspoon salt

For the crust: Preheat the oven to 350°F, and lightly grease a 9-inch springform pan. In a food processor or in a bag with a rolling pin, crush the graham crackers into fine crumbs. In a bowl, stir together the graham cracker crumbs, sugar, and melted butter. Pour into the prepared pan, and press the mixture evenly into the bottom and up the sides of the pan.

For the filling: In a large bowl, beat together the cream cheese and sugar until fluffy. In a bowl, whisk together the milk, eggs, and vanilla. Slowly add the milk mixture to the cream cheese mixture, and beat until smooth. Add the sour cream, and mix well. Add the sifted flour, salt, and lemon zest, and stir until well blended.

Pour the filling into your prepared crust and spread evenly. Bake for 1 hour and then turn the oven off. Leave the cake in the oven without opening the door for 4 hours to cool.

For the blackberry topping: In a saucepan, stir together the blackberries, sugar, lemon juice, cornstarch, and salt. Cook over medium heat until the mixture is thick and bubbling, about 10 minutes. Remove from the heat and cool. Once you take the cake out of the oven, spread the topping over the top. Chill in the refrigerator for at least 3 hours. Cut into wedges to serve.

BROWNIE CHEESECAKE

I visited New York City once and spent the entire trip touring bakeries around the city with my cousins. One of the treats that most stuck with me was a cheesecake with actual chunks of brownies folded in. That's what I've recreated here!

For the crust: In a food processor or in a bag with a rolling pin, crush the graham crackers into fine crumbs. In a bowl, mix together the butter and graham cracker crumbs until the butter has been fully incorporated. Press the mixture evenly in the bottom and up the sides of a 9-inch springform pan.

For the filling: Preheat the oven to 350°F. Cut your brownies into ½-inch cubes and set aside. In a large bowl, mix together the cream cheese, sour cream, and sugar. Beat in the eggs, one at a time, until completely incorporated. Stir in the vanilla and salt. Stir in the flour. Reserve 4 to 5 brownie cubes for the top of the cheesecake, and gently fold the rest of the brownie cubes into the filling.

Pour the filling into the prepared crust and spread evenly. Bake for 1 hour, and then turn the oven off. The cheesecake will be golden around the top edges. Leave the cheesecake in the oven for 3 hours to cool, then chill overnight in the refrigerator.

For the chocolate topping: In a small heatproof bowl, heat up the cream in the microwave until it's boiling. Add in the chocolate chips, and whisk until smooth. Pour the chocolate mixture over the top of the cheesecake, and place the reserved brownie cubes in the center. Cut into wedges and serve.

MAKES 10 TO 12 SERVINGS

FOR THE CRUST

16 graham crackers

6 tablespoons unsalted butter, softened

FOR THE FILLING

1 batch Classic Brownies (see page 174)

3 packages (8 ounces *each*) cream cheese, softened

½ cup sour cream

1 cup sugar

4 eggs

1 teaspoon vanilla extract

½ teaspoon salt

¼ cup all-purpose flour

FOR THE CHOCOLATE TOPPING

½ cup heavy cream

¾ cup dark chocolate chips

COOKIES

BAKERY-STYLE SUGAR COOKIES

These are classic, bakery-style sugar cookies. The outside
is crusted with big sugar chunks, and the inside is
soft and chewy—all the best qualities in sugar cookies.

Preheat the oven to 350°F and line 2 baking sheets
with parchment paper or nonstick mats. In a bowl,
whisk together the flour, baking soda, cream of
tartar, and salt. In a large bowl, beat together
the butter and sugar until fluffy. Add the egg
yolks, vanilla, and almond extracts, and beat until
combined. Slowly add the flour mixture and beat
until well mixed.

Scoop out the dough in roughly 2-tablespoon portions
and roll them into balls with your hands. Roll the
tops in the raw sugar. Place the balls on the prepared
baking sheets about 2 inches apart. Bake until
the cookies just begin to brown on the edges, 12 to
13 minutes—do not overbake! Cool slightly on the
pan before transferring to a cooling rack.

MAKES ABOUT 24 COOKIES

2½ cups plus 2 tablespoons
    all-purpose flour

1 teaspoon baking soda

½ teaspoon cream of tartar

¼ teaspoon salt

1 cup unsalted butter, softened

1¼ cups granulated sugar

3 egg yolks

1 tablespoon vanilla extract

1 teaspoon almond extract

¼ cup raw or coarse sugar

CHOCOLATE SUGAR COOKIES

These striking dark-chocolate cookies are super simple to make.
Rolling them in sugar before baking gives you a crunchy exterior,
while the inside stays chewy and light.

MAKES ABOUT 24 COOKIES

2 cups all-purpose flour

¾ cup dark cocoa powder

½ teaspoon baking soda

¼ teaspoon baking powder

½ teaspoon salt

¼ teaspoon ground cinnamon

14 tablespoons unsalted butter, melted

1 cup firmly packed brown sugar

¾ cup granulated sugar, plus more for rolling

1½ tablespoons strongly brewed coffee, cooled

1 teaspoon vanilla extract

1 whole egg

1 egg yolk

Preheat the oven to 350°F and line 2 baking sheets with parchment paper or nonstick mats. In a bowl, whisk together the flour, cocoa powder, baking soda, baking powder, salt, and cinnamon. In a large bowl, beat together the melted butter, brown sugar, and granulated sugar. Mix in the coffee, vanilla, whole egg, and egg yolk. Slowly add the flour mixture, and stir until completely combined.

Scoop rounded tablespoonfuls of the dough into your hands, and roll into balls. Then roll each ball in granulated sugar to coat it completely. Place on your baking sheets, and press down each dough ball slightly with the bottom of a glass. Space each cookie about 2 inches apart. Bake until the cookies are set and have cracks on the edges and top, 8 to 10 minutes. Transfer to a cooling rack to cool completely.

PRESSED SPICE COOKIES

These cookies, filled with warm, wintery spices, are pressed
with a cookie stamp to give them a beautiful design and flat shape.
If you don't have a cookie stamp, you can also use the
bottom of a drinking glass to achieve the same effect.

For the cookies: Preheat the oven to 350°F and line
2 baking sheets with parchment paper or nonstick
mats. In a bowl, stir together the flour, baking
powder, cinnamon, salt, allspice, and nutmeg. In
a large bowl, beat together the butter, granulated
sugar, and brown sugar until fluffy. Beat in the egg
and vanilla. Slowly add the flour mixture, and mix
until combined. The mixture will be crumbly. Add the
milk, 1 tablespoon at a time, until the dough comes
together. Use only as much milk as you need for the
dough to form.

For the coating: In a small bowl, stir together the
granulated sugar, coarse sugar, and cinnamon.

Scoop out the dough in roughly 2-tablespoon portions
and roll into balls with your hands. Then roll each
ball in the coating to coat it completely, and place
onto your baking sheets. Using a cookie stamp or the
back of a glass, press down until the dough is about
¼ inch thick. Bake until the cookies are golden on
the edges, 10 to 12 minutes. Let cool on a wire rack
before serving.

MAKES ABOUT 24 COOKIES

FOR THE COOKIES

3⅓ cups all-purpose flour

1¾ teaspoons baking powder

1 teaspoon ground cinnamon

½ teaspoon salt

½ teaspoon ground allspice

¼ teaspoon ground nutmeg

1 cup unsalted butter, softened

1 cup granulated sugar

¼ cup firmly packed brown sugar

1 egg

2 teaspoons vanilla extract

1 to 3 tablespoons whole milk,
    as needed

FOR THE COATING

½ cup granulated sugar

1 tablespoon coarse sugar

½ teaspoon ground cinnamon

OATMEAL, CHOCOLATE CHIP & ESPRESSO COOKIES

Oatmeal cookies are my favorite kind of cookies. The addition of blended oats here makes the cookies more substantial and, well, cookie-like. (Side-note: they may be my favorite cookies because they're the best cookie dough to eat raw.* I don't know why, but oatmeal cookie dough is insanely good.) If you don't like the flavor of coffee, you can omit the espresso powder and replace the brewed espresso with whole milk.

MAKES ABOUT 24 COOKIES

1 cup unsalted butter, softened

1 cup granulated sugar

1 cup firmly packed brown sugar

2 eggs

1 tablespoon strongly brewed espresso, cooled

1 teaspoon vanilla extract

3 cups old-fashioned rolled oats

2 cups all-purpose flour

1 teaspoon espresso powder

1 teaspoon baking powder

1 teaspoon baking soda

½ teaspoon salt

2 cups dark chocolate chips

Preheat the oven to 350°F and line 2 baking sheets with parchment paper or nonstick mats. In a large bowl, beat together the butter, granulated sugar, and brown sugar until fluffy. Add the eggs, espresso, and vanilla, and mix until well blended. In a food processor or blender, blend 2½ cups of the oats into a rough powder. Leave the remaining ½ cup whole.

In a bowl, stir together the blended oats, whole oats, flour, espresso powder, baking powder, baking soda, and salt. Slowly add the flour mixture to the butter mixture until it is completely incorporated. Stir in the chocolate chips.

Scoop 2-tablespoon portions of the cookie dough onto your baking sheets, with space between each cookie to allow for spreading. Press the dough down slightly and bake until the cookies are golden brown on the edges, 10 to 12 minutes. Transfer to a cooling rack to cool completely.

*Disclaimer: I cannot vouch for the safety of eating raw eggs in your cookie dough!

CLASSIC SHORTBREAD COOKIES

Shortbread cookies are light, buttery, and not too sweet. For me, they become addictive in a hurry, but luckily, they are super easy to make! You can use your favorite cookie cutters to make the cutest little shapes.

In a bowl, beat together the butter and powdered sugar until smooth. Beat in the vanilla and lemon extracts. Beat in the flour and salt until a soft dough forms.

Divide the dough in half, and form each half into a disk. Wrap each disk in plastic wrap and chill in the refrigerator for 30 to 45 minutes. (I know chilling dough is a drag, but it does matter for this one, I promise!)

Preheat the oven to 325°F and line a baking sheet with parchment paper or a nonstick mat. Using a rolling pin, on a lightly floured work surface, roll one dough disk between ¼ and ½ inch thick, and cut into your desired shapes. Repeat with the second disk. Using a metal spatula, transfer the cookies to the prepared pan. Bake until the cookie edges are just golden, 10 to 12 minutes. Let cool on a wire rack before serving.

SERVINGS VARY, DEPENDING ON THE SIZE OF YOUR CUTTER

1½ cups unsalted butter, softened

1 cup powdered sugar

2 teaspoons vanilla extract

½ teaspoon lemon extract

3¼ cups all-purpose flour

½ teaspoon salt

CHOCOLATE-DIPPED SHORTBREAD COOKIES

This is just a way to class up some shortbread cookies. Not only do you have the buttery, light shortbread, but you also get a coating of sweet chocolate to make everything better. I usually top these with sprinkles, crushed nuts, crushed-up candy canes, or mini chocolate chips, but use whatever toppings you prefer!

SERVINGS VARY DEPENDING ON THE SIZE OF YOUR CUTTER

1 cup dark or semisweet chocolate chips, melted (see page 16)

1 cup white chocolate chips, melted (see page 16)

Sprinkles and toppings of your choice (see note above)

1 batch Classic Shortbread Cookies, baked (see page 155)

Put the melted chocolates and toppings in separate bowls. Line a baking sheet with parchment paper.

Dip, brush, or drizzle each cookie into the chocolate of your choice and place on the baking sheet. While the chocolate is still wet, sprinkle with your toppings of choice. Allow the chocolate to set completely before serving.

JAM THUMBPRINT COOKIES

Thumbprint cookies remind me of childhood fun. These sweet
little guys can be filled with any jam you like, and they aren't
too sweet, so you can eat, like, 20 in one sitting. It's okay, I promise.

Line 2 baking sheets with parchment paper or
nonstick mats. In a large bowl, beat together the butter
and powdered sugar until light and fluffy. Add the
milk and vanilla, and mix well. Add the flour and
salt. Beat together until the ingredients are completely
incorporated, and the dough comes together.

Scoop the dough by rounded tablespoonfuls onto your
baking sheets. Use a ½-teaspoon measuring spoon to
press into each cookie, making a divot in the center
where the jam will go. Place the cookie dough in the
refrigerator for 30 minutes to chill.

Preheat the oven to 325°F. Take out the cookies,
and spoon the preserves into each divot, filling it
to the top of the indent. Bake until the cookies have
just started to brown, 20 to 22 minutes. Let cool
completely on a wire rack and enjoy.

MAKES ABOUT 30 COOKIES

1 cup unsalted butter, softened

⅔ cup powdered sugar

1 tablespoon whole milk

1 teaspoon vanilla extract

2 cups all-purpose flour

¼ teaspoon salt

½ cup raspberry jam (or whatever
jam you like)

SPICED CHOCOLATE SHORTBREAD COOKIES

There's just something about the combination of chocolate and warm spices that gets me in the holiday mood. These cookies are simple and provide both chocolate and spice, all wrapped up in one cookie.

MAKES ABOUT 24 COOKIES

1 cup unsalted butter, softened

⅓ cup firmly packed brown sugar

⅓ cup powdered sugar

1 teaspoon vanilla extract

1 teaspoon ground cinnamon

¼ teaspoon ground nutmeg

⅛ teaspoon ground cloves

½ teaspoon salt

2 cups all-purpose flour

¼ cup dark cocoa powder

Preheat the oven to 350°F and line 2 baking sheets with parchment paper or nonstick mats. In a large bowl, beat the butter, brown sugar, and powdered sugar until fluffy. Add the vanilla, cinnamon, nutmeg, cloves, and salt. Slowly add the flour and cocoa powder and mix well.

Put the dough on a lightly floured work surface. Using a rolling pin, roll out the dough to about ¼ inch thick. Cut into shapes with the cookie cutters of your choice. Bake until the dough looks dry, 8 to 10 minutes. Let cool on a wire rack and enjoy.

CLASSIC CHOCOLATE CHIP–WALNUT COOKIES

It's an important life skill to be able to make your favorite kind of chocolate chip cookie, and this is mine. The texture is just right, and the results are hearty, chewy, and crunchy on the edges.

Preheat the oven to 350°F and line 2 baking sheets with parchment or nonstick mats. In a bowl, stir together the flour, cornstarch, baking soda, salt, and cinnamon. In a large bowl, beat together the butter, brown sugar, and granulated sugar until fluffy. Beat in the eggs and vanilla until smooth. Slowly add the flour mixture until well mixed. Fold in the dark and semisweet chocolate chips and the walnuts.

Scoop 2-tablespoon portions onto your baking sheets. Bake until the edges of the cookies are slightly golden, 8 to 10 minutes. Let the cookies cool on wire racks and dig in.

MAKES ABOUT 36 COOKIES

4 cups all-purpose flour

¼ cup cornstarch

2 teaspoons baking soda

½ teaspoon salt

½ teaspoon ground cinnamon

1½ cups unsalted butter, softened

1½ cups firmly packed brown sugar

½ cup granulated sugar

2 eggs

1 tablespoon vanilla extract

1 cup dark chocolate chips

½ cup semisweet mini chocolate chips

1 cup chopped walnuts, toasted

HONEY-ROSEMARY SHORTBREAD COOKIES

It might be hard to think about rosemary in a cookie, and I'm not gonna lie, it takes some time to grow on you. But after you've had a cookie or two, they become completely addictive. Plus, it seems kinda fun and trendy to stick herbs in everything.

MAKES 30 TO 35 COOKIES

FOR THE COOKIES

1½ cups unsalted butter, softened

1 cup powdered sugar

1 teaspoon vanilla extract

⅓ cup honey

3½ cups all-purpose flour

½ teaspoon salt

3 teaspoons ground dried rosemary

FOR THE ICING

1 cup powdered sugar

¼ cup honey

1 tablespoon whole milk

¼ teaspoon ground dried rosemary

⅛ teaspoon salt

For the cookies: In a large bowl, beat together the butter and powdered sugar until fluffy. Beat in the vanilla and honey. Add in the flour, salt, and rosemary, and beat until fully mixed. The dough will be soft. Divide the dough in half, and form one half into a log on top of a large sheet of plastic wrap. You don't have to make it perfectly round! Wrap the log in the plastic wrap. Repeat with the second half of the dough. Refrigerate the logs for 20 minutes. Take the logs out of the fridge and roll them into smoother cylinders. Keep the dough wrapped as you shape it, and then chill until the dough is very firm, 30 minutes.

Preheat the oven to 325°F and line 2 baking sheets with parchment paper or nonstick mats. Remove 1 roll of dough and cut it into slices about ¼ inch thick. Evenly space the slices on one of your baking sheets, and place the baking sheet in the refrigerator for about 10 minutes. Place the baking sheet directly into the preheated oven, and bake until the cookies are just golden on the edges, 8 to 10 minutes. Repeat the process of slicing and chilling before baking each batch of cookies. Let cool completely before icing.

For the icing: In a bowl, mix the powdered sugar, honey, milk, rosemary, and salt until smooth. Transfer to a plastic bag or piping bag with a thin tip. Drizzle the icing over your cooled cookies. Let the icing set before serving.

OATMEAL COOKIE THINS

This version of the classic oatmeal cookie bakes up thin and develops crispy edges and a chewy center as it cools. It's not as hearty as its older brother, the regular oatmeal cookie, but it has an enticing texture that I keep coming back to. These cookies are also great with tea, if you're feeling classy.

Preheat the oven to 350°F and line 2 baking sheets with parchment paper or nonstick mats. In a bowl, stir together the oats, flour, cinnamon, baking soda, baking powder, and salt. In a large bowl, beat together the butter, granulated sugar, and brown sugar until fluffy. Add the egg and vanilla, and stir until combined. Slowly add the flour mixture. Make sure to mix the dough thoroughly, ensuring an even consistency throughout.

Scoop the dough onto your baking sheets in mounds of 1 to 2 tablespoonfuls. Lightly press down on the mounds to flatten. Bake until the cookies are just golden on the edges, 10 to 12 minutes. Let cool completely on the wire racks. The cookies will become crisper as they cool, remaining chewy in the centers.

MAKES ABOUT 24 COOKIES

2 cups old-fashioned rolled oats

1¾ cups all-purpose flour

1 teaspoon ground cinnamon

½ teaspoon baking soda

⅛ teaspoon baking powder

½ teaspoon salt

1 cup unsalted butter, softened

1 cup granulated sugar

½ cup firmly packed brown sugar

1 egg

2 teaspoons vanilla extract

OATMEAL, WHITE CHOCOLATE & CRANBERRY COOKIES

Raisins aren't my jam, but dried cranberries are great in every way—they are more flavorful than their dried grape cousins, a prettier color, and perfect when tucked inside an oatmeal cookie. These are totally the flavors of fall, in case you were wondering.

MAKES ABOUT 36 COOKIES

1 cup unsalted butter, softened

1 cup granulated sugar

1 cup firmly packed brown sugar

2 eggs

1 teaspoon vanilla extract

2¾ cups old-fashioned rolled oats, blended or processed to a rough powder

2 cups all-purpose flour

1 teaspoon baking soda

1 teaspoon baking powder

½ teaspoon salt

½ teaspoon ground cinnamon

1 cup white chocolate chips

1 cup chopped dried cranberries

Preheat the oven to 350°F and line 2 baking sheets with parchment paper or nonstick mats. In a bowl, beat together the butter, granulated sugar, and brown sugar until fluffy. Add the eggs and vanilla and mix well. In another bowl, mix the oatmeal, flour, baking soda, baking powder, salt, and cinnamon. Slowly beat the flour mixture into the butter mixture until completely combined. Fold in the chocolate chips and cranberries.

Scoop rough mounds of approximately 2 tablespoons onto your prepared baking sheets, with space between each mound to allow for spreading. Bake until the tops are just starting to brown, 8 to 10 minutes. Do not overbake! Let cool on a wire rack before serving.

FUNFETTI MERINGUES

You know how sometimes you need egg yolks for a recipe,
and then you've got sad, lonely egg whites sitting around?
Pair them with sprinkles in these meringues, and they'll be so happy!

Preheat the oven to 200°F and line a baking sheet
with parchment paper or a nonstick mat. In a large
bowl, combine the egg whites and cream of tartar.
Using a stand mixer or a hand mixer, whip until the
mixture is foamy and has started to thicken. While
continuing to beat, slowly add the sugar in a thin,
steady stream. Continue beating until the mixture
is glossy and opaque, and has soft but sturdy peaks.
After you add the sugar, it's hard to overwhip these,
but you want them to be very thick. Mix in the vanilla
and almond extracts. Fold in the sprinkles until just
combined.

Using a medium ice cream scoop, or a large spoon,
scoop the meringue evenly onto your baking sheet.
These do not spread while baking, so you can put
them close together. Scatter more sprinkles over
the tops of the meringues. Bake for 1 hour—the
cookies should look dry on top—and then turn the
oven off and leave the meringues in the oven for
1 hour longer. Remove from the oven and let cool
completely before serving.

MAKES ABOUT 16 MERINGUES

4 egg whites

¼ teaspoon cream of tartar

1 cup sugar

½ teaspoon vanilla extract

½ teaspoon almond extract

½ cup rainbow sprinkles,
  plus more for garnish

BARS

CLASSIC BROWNIES

Brownies are a bit of a mystery—how do you get that crunchy, flaky top layer while keeping the bottom fudgy and soft? Well, this recipe achieves just that, plus the dark chocolate flavor is everything you'll ever need in a brownie.

MAKES 8 TO 12 BROWNIES

⅔ cup vegetable oil

¾ cup dark cocoa powder

⅔ cup all-purpose flour

½ teaspoon salt

⅛ teaspoon baking powder

3 eggs

1 cup granulated sugar

⅔ cup firmly packed brown sugar

1 teaspoon vanilla extract

1 teaspoon espresso powder

½ cup semisweet chocolate chunks

Preheat the oven to 350°F and grease an 8-inch square baking pan. In a small bowl, whisk together the oil and cocoa powder until smooth. In a bowl, whisk together the flour, salt, and baking powder. In a large bowl, beat together the eggs, granulated sugar, brown sugar, vanilla, and espresso powder until smooth. Stir the cocoa mixture into the egg mixture until completely incorporated. Then stir in the flour mixture and mix well. Fold in the chocolate chunks.

Pour the batter into your prepared pan, spreading it out evenly. Bake until the brownies have set, 25 to 30 minutes. Let cool on a wire rack before removing from the pan, then cut into squares and serve.

RASPBERRY CHEESECAKE BROWNIES

You thought cheesecake brownies were enough, right? But no, raspberry cheesecake brownies, those are enough. These are tart, chocolatey, and cheesecake-filled, so stop reading and make them!

For the raspberry sauce: In a small saucepan, cook the raspberries, sugar, and cornstarch over medium-low heat until soft and sauce-like, about 10 minutes. Let cool completely.

For the brownies: Preheat the oven to 325°F. Grease a 9-by-13-inch baking pan and line with parchment paper cut to fit. In a saucepan, melt together the butter, chocolate, and cocoa powder, stirring until smooth. Let the mixture cool completely in the pan. Once the chocolate mixture is cooled, stir in the sugar. Then stir in the eggs, one at a time, and the vanilla. Finally, stir in the flour and salt until combined. Transfer the batter to the prepared pan, using a rubber spatula to scrape it all out of the saucepan, and spread the batter evenly into the pan.

For the filling: In a bowl, beat together the cream cheese and sour cream. Add the sugar, and beat well. Add the egg, flour, and vanilla, and beat until the mixture is very smooth.

Dollop the filling all over the top of your brownie batter. Using a knife, swirl the mixtures together to create a marbled effect. Then drizzle the raspberry sauce over the top, and swirl again. Bake until completely set, or until a cake tester inserted about 2 inches from the edge comes out clean, 40 to 45 minutes. Let cool completely on a wire rack before removing from the pan, and cut into squares to serve.

MAKES 15 TO 18 BROWNIES

FOR THE RASPBERRY SAUCE

1 pint raspberries

2 tablespoons sugar

2 tablespoons cornstarch

FOR THE BROWNIES

1 cup unsalted butter

4 ounces unsweetened chocolate, chopped

1 tablespoon cocoa powder

2 cups sugar

4 eggs

1 tablespoon vanilla extract

¾ cup all-purpose flour

1 teaspoon salt

FOR THE FILLING

1 package (8 ounces) cream cheese, softened

¼ cup sour cream

½ cup sugar

1 egg

2 tablespoons all-purpose flour

1 teaspoon vanilla extract

PEANUT BUTTER BROWNIES

Peanut butter and chocolate go together—we know this.
So is it any surprise that putting the good stuff together in
brownie form is perfection in a pan? Nah, no surprise.

MAKES 8 TO 12 BROWNIES

½ cup unsalted butter

2 ounces unsweetened chocolate,
chopped

1 cup sugar

2 eggs

1 teaspoon vanilla extract

½ cup plus 2 tablespoons
peanut butter chips

¼ cup all-purpose flour

2 tablespoons dark cocoa powder

½ teaspoon salt

⅓ cup crunchy peanut butter

Preheat the oven to 325°F and coat an 8-inch square cake pan with cooking spray. In a saucepan over medium-low heat, melt the butter and chocolate and whisk until smooth. Remove from the heat, pour the mixture into a large bowl, and let cool for 10 minutes. Stir in the sugar, eggs, and vanilla. Then stir in ½ cup of the peanut butter chips, the flour, cocoa powder, and salt. Pour the batter into your prepared cake pan, spreading it out evenly.

Put the peanut butter in a small bowl and place in the microwave. Cook on full power in short bursts until it's very pliable and has a similar texture to the brownie batter (it usually takes me about 45 to 60 seconds or so). Spoon the peanut butter evenly across the top of the batter, and use a knife to swirl it into the batter to create a marbled effect. Sprinkle the remaining 2 tablespoons peanut butter chips over the top.

Bake until a cake tester placed about an inch in from the side of the pan comes out clean, about 35 minutes. Let the brownies cool slightly on a wire rack before removing from the pan. Cut into squares to serve.

SUGAR COOKIE BARS

I'm generally pretty vanilla, and sugar cookies are one of my favorite things of all time. I know they are simple, but sometimes simple is best. This bar version of the classic treat is soft, sweet, and topped with a smooth buttercream for extra fun. Sprinkles are necessary, yes.

For the cookie bars: Preheat the oven to 350°F and grease a 9-by-13-inch baking pan. In a bowl, whisk together the flour, salt, baking powder, and baking soda. In a large bowl, beat together the butter, oil, granulated sugar, and powdered sugar until fluffy. Beat in the egg, water, vanilla, and almond extract. Slowly add the flour mixture, and stir until completely combined. Fold in the confetti sprinkles. Spread the dough evenly in your prepared pan. Bake until the cookie bars are firm and look just golden near the edges, 14 to 16 minutes. Let cool completely on a wire rack before removing them from the pan and frosting.

For the frosting: In a bowl, beat together the butter, powdered sugar, vanilla, almond extract, and salt until blended and thick. Beat in the cream until the mixture becomes fluffy. Fold in 2 tablespoons of the sprinkles.

Spread the frosting over the cooled bars, and top with the remaining 1 tablespoon sprinkles. Cut the bars into rectangles and enjoy.

MAKES 15 TO 18 BARS

FOR THE COOKIE BARS

3 cups all-purpose flour

½ teaspoon salt

½ teaspoon baking powder

⅛ teaspoon baking soda

½ cup unsalted butter, softened

¼ cup plus 2 tablespoons vegetable oil

¾ cup granulated sugar

¼ cup powdered sugar

1 egg

3 tablespoons water

2 teaspoons vanilla extract

1 teaspoon almond extract

¼ cup confetti sprinkles

FOR THE FROSTING

1 cup unsalted butter, softened

3 cups powdered sugar

1 teaspoon vanilla extract

½ teaspoon almond extract

¼ teaspoon salt

2 tablespoons heavy cream

3 tablespoons confetti sprinkles

SALTED CARAMEL BLONDIES

These blondies have big craters of caramel dotting the top and
salt flecks speckled all around. They are chewy and salty
and pretty much take care of all your cravings at once.

MAKES 15 TO 18 BLONDIES

1 cup unsalted butter, softened

1¾ cups firmly packed brown sugar

4 eggs

2 teaspoons vanilla extract

1 cup all-purpose flour

1 teaspoon salt

1 cup dark chocolate chips

3 tablespoons Caramel Sauce
(see page 227)

Coarse salt

Preheat the oven to 325°F and grease a 9-by-13-inch
baking pan. In a bowl, beat together the butter and
brown sugar until fluffy. Mix in the eggs and vanilla.
Stir in the flour and salt until completely combined.
Then stir in the chocolate chips. Spread the mixture
evenly into your prepared pan. Drizzle the caramel
sauce over the top, and sprinkle lightly with coarse
salt over the top as well.

Bake until the bars have set and are golden brown,
35 to 40 minutes. Let cool on a wire rack before
removing from the pan, and then cut into rectangles
to serve.

BERRY-LEMON CRUMB BARS

I used to work at a coffee shop, and they served something
like these berry-lemon crumb bars—I was obsessed. I like a mixture
of blackberries, raspberries, and blueberries, but you do you!

For the crust: Preheat the oven to 350°F. Line a 9-by-13-inch baking pan with foil and grease the foil. In a bowl, beat together the butter and powdered sugar, then add the vanilla and salt. Slowly add the flour to make a dough. Press the dough into your lined pan to coat evenly the bottom of the pan. Bake until lightly golden, about 10 minutes, then cool. Leave the oven set at 350°F.

For the berries: Place the berries, cornstarch, granulated sugar, and lemon juice in a small saucepan. Cook over medium heat until the berries have softened. Puree the mixture in a food processor or blender just until chunky, not completely smooth. Pour the berry mixture over the cooled crust and spread evenly.

For the lemon filling: In a bowl, whisk together the eggs, granulated sugar, lemon zest, juice, flour, and sour cream until completely smooth. Pour the mixture over the crust and berries, and bake until just bubbling, about 10 minutes.

For the crumb: In a bowl, mix together the flour, granulated sugar, and powdered sugar. Add the melted butter and stir with a fork until crumbs form, adding more butter if needed. After the bars have baked for 10 minutes, pull them out of the oven and sprinkle the crumb topping over the top. Return to the oven, and bake until the lemon filling is just slightly jiggly in the center, 35 to 40 minutes. Let cool completely on a wire rack before removing from the pan and cutting and eating.

MAKES 15 TO 18 BARS

FOR THE CRUST

1 cup unsalted butter, softened

⅔ cup powdered sugar

2 teaspoons vanilla extract

¼ teaspoon salt

2 cups all-purpose flour

FOR THE BERRIES

2 cups mixed berries

1 tablespoon cornstarch

1 tablespoon granulated sugar

Juice of ½ lemon

FOR THE LEMON FILLING

6 eggs

3 cups granulated sugar

Finely grated zest of 3 to 4 lemons

1 cup lemon juice
(from 5 to 6 lemons)

1 cup all-purpose flour

¼ cup sour cream

FOR THE CRUMB

½ cup all-purpose flour

½ cup granulated sugar

½ cup powdered sugar

3 tablespoons unsalted butter,
melted, plus more if needed

BLUEBERRY CHEESECAKE BARS

Making cheesecake is a pretty big undertaking. But making cheesecake bars is totally easy and manageable! Plus, if you get any cracks in the filling, it's okay—you'll be slathering blueberry sauce all over the top!

MAKES 8 TO 12 BARS

FOR THE CRUST

About 40 vanilla wafer cookies, crushed

2 tablespoons sugar

5 tablespoons unsalted butter, melted

FOR THE CREAM CHEESE FILLING

2 packages (8 ounces *each*) cream cheese, softened

¾ cup sugar

2 eggs

¼ cup sour cream

1 teaspoon vanilla extract

2 tablespoons all-purpose flour

½ teaspoon salt

2 tablespoons heavy cream

FOR THE BLUEBERRY TOPPING

2 pints blueberries

2 tablespoons sugar

1 tablespoon cornstarch

Finely grated zest and juice of 1 lemon

For the crust: Lightly grease an 8-inch square baking pan. Stir together the crushed cookies, sugar, and melted butter until evenly incorporated. Press the mixture into the bottom of the greased pan.

For the cream cheese filling: Preheat the oven to 350°F. In a large bowl, mix together the cream cheese and sugar until combined. Stir in the eggs, sour cream, and vanilla. Sift in the flour and salt, and stir together until blended. Add the cream, and stir well. Pour the mixture over the prepared crust. Bake until just golden and set, 30 to 35 minutes.

For the blueberry topping: In a saucepan, stir together the blueberries, sugar, cornstarch, lemon zest, and juice. Cook over medium heat, stirring frequently, until the mixture has thickened, about 5 minutes. Pour the blueberry mixture over the baked cream cheese filling while still warm. Cover with foil or plastic wrap and chill in the refrigerator for at least 2 to 3 hours before removing from the pan. Cut into squares and serve.

CHAI-SPICED COOKIE BARS

The first time I tried chai was a magical experience. There's something really comforting about the mixture of tea with such deeply flavored spices. These bars are a pretty cozy sidekick, and there's actual chai tea ground up and mixed right in!

For the bars: Preheat the oven to 350°F and grease a 9-by-13-inch baking pan. In a bowl, whisk together the flour, salt, baking powder, and baking soda. Cut open the tea bags and empty the contents into a spice grinder or blender. Blend until it is a fine powder. Whisk the tea powder into the flour mixture.

In a large bowl, beat together the butter, granulated sugar, and powdered sugar until fluffy. Mix in the egg, cream, and vanilla. Slowly stir in the flour mixture, and mix until completely blended. Spread the dough evenly in the prepared pan. Bake until lightly golden brown and set, 14 to 16 minutes. Let cool completely in the pan on a wire rack before removing and icing.

For the icing: In a bowl, mix together the powdered sugar and 4 tablespoons of the cream until blended. Cut open the tea bags and empty the contents into the spice grinder or blender. Blend to a fine powder, then mix the powder into the sugar mixture. Add more cream if needed to reach your desired consistency. Drizzle the icing over the bars. Cut into rectangles and serve.

MAKES 15 TO 18 BARS

FOR THE BARS

3 cups all-purpose flour

½ teaspoon salt

½ teaspoon baking powder

⅛ teaspoon baking soda

6 standard-size chai-spiced black tea bags

1 cup unsalted butter, softened

¾ cup granulated sugar

¼ cup powdered sugar

1 egg

¼ cup heavy cream

2 teaspoons vanilla extract

FOR THE ICING

1 cup powdered sugar

4 to 5 tablespoons heavy cream

2 standard-size chai-spiced black tea bags

BUTTERSCOTCH BARS

Butterscotch is one of those things that I get a lot of requests for
on my blog. These bars are a lot like a traditional chocolate chip cookie,
but the addition of oats adds a bit more depth and texture.

MAKES 15 TO 18 BARS

2 cups all-purpose flour

½ cup old-fashioned oats

1 tablespoon cornstarch

¾ teaspoon baking powder

½ teaspoon salt

1 cup unsalted butter, softened

1¼ cups firmly packed brown sugar

¾ cup granulated sugar

2 eggs

1 teaspoon vanilla extract

1½ cups butterscotch chips

Preheat the oven to 350°F and grease a 9-by-13-inch baking pan. In a bowl, whisk together the flour, oats, cornstarch, baking powder, and salt. In a large bowl, beat together the butter, brown sugar, and granulated sugar until fluffy. Beat in the eggs and vanilla. Slowly add the flour mixture until completely incorporated. Stir in the butterscotch chips. Spread the dough evenly in the prepared pan.

Bake until the bars are golden and set, 30 to 35 minutes. Let cool on a wire rack before removing from the pan and cut into rectangles to serve.

TOASTED MARSHMALLOW & RICE CEREAL BARS

These bars are a combination of a cookie bar and a rice cereal bar, all with the flavor of toasted marshmallows folded right in. You can actually toast marshmallows on the stovetop, by the way—even an electric stove does the trick!

To toast the marshmallows, use a fork or a wooden skewer to hold the marshmallows over your stove burner, turned to medium-high heat, turning to toast evenly. This works on electric stoves as well as gas!

Preheat the oven to 350°F, and grease a 13-by-18-inch jelly roll pan or rimmed baking sheet. In a bowl, whisk together the flour, cornstarch, baking soda, salt, and cinnamon. In a large bowl, beat together the butter, brown sugar, and granulated sugar until fluffy. Beat in the eggs and vanilla. Slowly add the flour mixture to the butter mixture, and mix until combined. Stir in the rice cereal and toasted marshmallows (they will break apart as you mix them) until evenly combined. Evenly press the dough into your jelly roll pan.

Bake until the sides of the bars are golden and the center is puffy, 12 to 15 minutes. Let cool completely on a wire rack before removing from the pan and cutting into squares.

MAKES ABOUT 24 BARS

1 cup standard-size marshmallows (stuff them in the cup!)

4 cups all-purpose flour

¼ cup cornstarch

2 teaspoons baking soda

1½ teaspoons salt

½ teaspoon ground cinnamon

1½ cups unsalted butter, softened

1½ cups firmly packed brown sugar

½ cup granulated sugar

2 eggs

2 teaspoons vanilla extract

2½ cups puffed rice cereal

CHOCOLATE CHUNK-HAZELNUT BARS

You like chocolate-hazelnut spread, right? I mean, if the answer is no, we need to talk. These are kind of like peanut butter cookies, but instead of peanut butter, you use that spread we all know and love. They're so good, you guys!

MAKES ABOUT 24 BARS

2¾ cups all-purpose flour

½ teaspoon baking soda

½ teaspoon baking powder

½ teaspoon ground cinnamon

½ teaspoon salt

¾ cup unsalted butter, softened

1 cup purchased chocolate-hazelnut spread

1 cup granulated sugar

1 cup firmly packed brown sugar

2 eggs

2 teaspoons vanilla extract

1 cup chocolate chunks

½ cup semisweet mini chocolate chips

Preheat the oven to 350°F. Lightly grease a 13-by-18-inch rimmed baking sheet, and line with a sheet of parchment paper cut to fit. In a bowl, whisk together the flour, baking soda, baking powder, cinnamon, and salt. In a large bowl, beat together the butter, chocolate-hazelnut spread, granulated sugar, and brown sugar until smooth. Beat in the eggs and vanilla. Slowly add the flour mixture, beating until completely combined. Fold in the chocolate chunks and mini chocolate chips until well incorporated. Spread the dough evenly in the prepared sheet pan, using an offset spatula.

Bake until the bars have set and are golden brown on top, 18 to 20 minutes. Let cool on a wire rack before removing from the pan, cut into rectangles, and enjoy.

PEACH-CHERRY PIE BARS

Bars are a pretty great choice when you need to feed a crowd, and these are no exception. Fresh cherries and peaches meet between layers of sweet, soft sugar cookie, and the results are pretty awesome.

Preheat the oven to 350°F, and grease a 9-by-13-inch baking pan. Line the pan with parchment paper cut to fit. In a bowl, whisk together the flour, baking powder, and salt. In a large bowl, beat 1¾ cups of the sugar and the butter together until fluffy. Beat in the eggs and vanilla. Press about two-thirds of this dough evenly into the bottom of the prepared pan. Bake until the dough is just barely turning golden on the edges, 8 to 10 minutes.

Meanwhile, in a saucepan over medium-high heat, combine the cherries, peaches, remaining ½ cup sugar, the cornstarch, lemon zest, and water. Cook the mixture, stirring occasionally, until thick.

Remove the partially baked crust from the oven. Spread the warm fruit mixture on top of the crust. Take the remaining dough and form small bits into flattened shapes. Place these bits evenly over the top, leaving some areas of fruit uncovered. Place back in the oven, and bake until the top dough bits are golden brown, 30 to 35 minutes. Let cool completely on a wire rack before removing from the pan and cutting into bars to serve.

MAKES 15 TO 18 BARS

3¼ cups all-purpose flour

1 teaspoon baking powder

1 teaspoon salt

2¼ cups sugar

1 cup unsalted butter, softened

3 eggs

1 teaspoon vanilla extract

2 cups cherries, pitted

2 large ripe peaches, peeled, pitted, and chopped

1½ tablespoons cornstarch

Finely grated zest of 1 lemon

3 tablespoons water

S'MORES BARS

There are two kinds of people—the kind who burn their marshmallows to a blackened crisp, lighting them completely on fire, and the kind who like a light golden color all around. Whichever you are, these s'mores bars deliver a sweet dessert with a dose of nostalgia. (I like 'em burned.)

MAKES 15 TO 18 BARS

2½ cups all-purpose flour

2 cups graham cracker crumbs

¾ teaspoon baking powder

1 teaspoon ground cinnamon

½ teaspoon salt

1 cup unsalted butter, softened

1½ cups firmly packed brown sugar

2 eggs

1 teaspoon vanilla extract

2 cups purchased marshmallow fluff

2 cups dark chocolate chips

Preheat the oven to 350°F. Grease a 9-by-13-inch baking pan and line with parchment paper cut to fit. In a bowl, stir together the flour, graham cracker crumbs, baking powder, cinnamon, and salt. In a large bowl, beat together the butter and brown sugar until fluffy. Add the eggs and vanilla and mix until combined. Slowly add the flour mixture, and mix until completely combined.

Press about three-quarters of the dough evenly onto the bottom of your prepared pan. Using an offset spatula, evenly spread the marshmallow fluff on top of the layer of dough. Sprinkle the chocolate chips evenly over the top of the marshmallow fluff.

Take a small chunk of the remaining dough and form it into a rough disk, and place it on top of the marshmallow. Repeat this process until all the dough has been used and the top of the bars is evenly coated with the disks, leaving a little room between each one for the marshmallow fluff to ooze through. Bake until the top dough bits are golden and the bars seem set, 35 to 40 minutes. Let cool on a wire rack before removing from the pan and cutting into rectangles to serve.

PIES, TARTS & COBBLERS

FLAKY PIE CRUST

Count this recipe as your go-to pastry crust. It is lightly sweet, reliably flaky, and super simple to make. Use it for pies and quiches and whatever else your stomach calls for!

MAKES TWO 9-INCH PIE CRUSTS

1 cup unsalted butter, chilled and cubed

¼ cup powdered sugar

1 egg beaten with 1 tablespoon cold water

2½ cups all-purpose flour

½ teaspoon salt

In a bowl, combine the butter and powdered sugar. Using a pastry blender, cut the butter into the sugar, leaving the butter in pretty large chunks. Pour in the egg mixture and stir to coat. Add the flour and salt, and use your pastry blender to cut in the ingredients until a dough starts to form. Then turn the dough onto a floured work surface, and form it into a rough ball. Divide the dough in half, and form each half into a disk. Wrap each disk in plastic wrap, and refrigerate for at least 30 minutes.

Unwrap one dough disk and place it on a lightly floured work surface. Using a rolling pin, and working from the center outwards in all directions, roll the dough into an 11-inch round. Turn the dough and re-flour the surface and pin as needed to prevent sticking. Carefully transfer the dough to a 9-inch pie dish, centering it in the dish. Trim the edges, if needed, and crimp the edges, if you like. If you're not using the second dough disk, place it in a locking plastic bag and refrigerate it for 2 to 3 days, or freeze it for up to 3 months. Thaw overnight in the refrigerator before using.

To partially bake your pie crust, preheat the oven to 350°F. Place a sheet of foil into the pie crust, easing it into the edges. Fill the foil with pie weights. Bake until the crust is dry and the foil easily separates, 15 to 20 minutes. Carefully remove the foil and pie weights from the crust and place the crust on a wire rack to cool.

To fully bake your pie crust, follow the instructions for partially baking, baking until the crust is a light golden color, 30 to 35 minutes.

TART CRUST

This is the crust I use for all of my sweet tart recipes,
and it's super simple. The result is a sturdy, sweet,
cookie-like crust that holds up to fillings of all kinds.

In a bowl, stir together the flour, powdered sugar, and
salt. Using a pastry blender, cut the cold butter into
the flour mixture until the mixture resembles coarse
crumbs. In a small bowl, beat together the egg and
vanilla. Add the egg mixture to the flour mixture,
and stir together until a dough starts to form. Turn
out the dough onto a floured work surface and form
the dough into a disk.

Using a rolling pin, and working from the center
outwards in all directions, roll the dough into a 12-
inch round. Turn the dough and re-flour the surface
and pin as needed to prevent sticking. Carefully
transfer the dough to a 10-inch tart pan with a
removable bottom, centering it in the pan.
Trim the edges flush to remove any excess dough.
Using a fork, poke several holes in the bottom of
the crust. Wrap the entire pan with plastic wrap
or foil and place in the freezer until completely
frozen, 30 to 45 minutes.

To partially bake your tart crust, preheat the oven
to 350°F. Unwrap the tart crust and place it into the
oven directly from the freezer, and bake until the
edges have just started to brown, 10 to 15 minutes.

To fully bake your tart crust, follow the instructions
for partially baking, baking until the crust is light
golden brown all over, 25 to 30 minutes.

MAKES ONE 10-INCH TART CRUST

1½ cups all-purpose flour

½ cup powdered sugar

½ teaspoon salt

¾ cup unsalted butter,
  chilled and cubed

1 egg

1 teaspoon vanilla extract

APPLE CRUMBLE PIE

A crumble topping is great pretty much wherever you put it, and this
pie is no exception. This is a classic apple pie topped with a sweet,
crunchy cinnamon crumble that will seriously warm your soul right up.

MAKES 8 SERVINGS

FOR THE FILLING

6 large Granny Smith apples

½ cup granulated sugar

¼ cup firmly packed brown sugar

3 tablespoons all-purpose flour

1 teaspoon vanilla extract

1 teaspoon ground cinnamon

½ teaspoon ground allspice

1 Flaky Pie Crust (see page 202),
   unbaked

FOR THE CRUMBLE TOPPING

½ cup all-purpose flour

½ cup chopped pecans

¼ cup granulated sugar

⅓ cup firmly packed brown sugar

½ teaspoon ground cinnamon

¼ teaspoon salt

6 tablespoons unsalted butter,
   softened

Whiskey Vanilla Ice Cream
   (see page 231) for serving

For the filling: Preheat the oven to 350°F. Peel and
core your apples, and thinly slice them. I slice the
apples, whole, cut out the cores, and then cut each
slice in half. However, you can use any method you
prefer, as long as you end up with thin, even slices.
In a large bowl, toss together the apples, granulated
sugar, brown sugar, flour, vanilla, cinnamon, and
allspice until all the apples are evenly coated.

Pour the filling into your crust, and arrange it evenly.

For the crumble topping: In a bowl, stir together
the flour, pecans, granulated sugar, brown sugar,
cinnamon, and salt. Using a spoon or your hands,
cut in the softened butter until crumbles form.
Sprinkle the mixture evenly on top of your pie.

Bake until the crust and toppings are golden
brown and the filling is bubbling underneath,
40 to 50 minutes. Let cool slightly on a wire rack.
Cut into wedges and serve warm, with some Whiskey
Vanilla Ice Cream.

LEMON MERINGUE PIE

My grandma used to make perfect lemon meringue pies for birthdays, or so I hear. I've tried meringue pies many times, and they just aren't easy. But I think I've figured it out with this recipe, even if the one my grandma left doesn't seem to work in my own kitchen!

For the filling: In a large saucepan, whisk together the sugar, water, lemon juice, cornstarch, lemon zest, egg yolks, and salt. Slowly stir in the boiling water. Cook the mixture over medium heat until thickened, about 10 minutes. Remove from the heat, and whisk in the butter.

Pour the thickened mixture into your prepared pie crust. Sprinkle the breadcrumbs evenly over the top of the filling.

For the meringue: In a double boiler or a large heatproof bowl placed over (but not touching) a pot of boiling water, use a handheld mixer to whisk together the egg whites and sugar until the mixture reaches 160°F on an instant-read thermometer, or until the sugar is completely dissolved. Remove from the heat and beat on medium speed for 10 to 15 minutes. The mixture should be light, fluffy, and completely cooled, with stiff peaks. Stir in the vanilla and salt.

Preheat the oven to 200°F. Scoop the meringue onto the prepared filling and spread all the way to the edges of the pie dish. Using a fork, fluff the meringue to give it a few peaks. Bake for 15 minutes and then turn the oven to a low broil setting. Keep a close eye on the pie, and bake until the meringue is lightly toasted on top, especially on the peaks. Remove and cool on the counter until room temperature, then chill in the refrigerator for several hours before cutting into wedges and serving.

MAKES 8 SERVINGS

FOR THE FILLING

1 cup sugar

⅔ cup water

⅔ cup lemon juice

⅓ cup cornstarch

1 tablespoon finely grated lemon zest

4 egg yolks

1 teaspoon salt

1 cup boiling water

2 tablespoons unsalted butter

1 Flaky Pie Crust (see page 202), fully baked

1 tablespoon dried breadcrumbs

FOR THE MERINGUE

6 egg whites

1¼ cups sugar

1 teaspoon vanilla extract

¼ teaspoon salt

BROWNIE PIE

This pie is kind of like a brownie sundae, but without the ice cream. Although you could add ice cream—I bet that would be amazing! Anyway, think flaky pie crust, fudgy brownies, whipped cream, and toppings. So good!

MAKES 8 TO 10 SERVINGS

FOR THE FILLING

½ cup unsalted butter

2 ounces unsweetened chocolate, chopped

1 cup sugar

2 eggs

1 teaspoon vanilla extract

½ cup dark chocolate chips

⅓ cup all-purpose flour

¼ teaspoon salt

1 Flaky Pie Crust (see page 202), partially baked

FOR THE TOPPING

1½ cups heavy cream

¼ cup Caramel Sauce (see page 227)

1 to 2 tablespoons purchased fudge sauce

For the filling: Preheat the oven to 325°F. In a saucepan, melt together the butter and unsweetened chocolate, stirring until smooth. Remove from the heat and let cool for 10 minutes. Stir in the sugar until mixed. Stir in the eggs and vanilla until combined. Add the chocolate chips, flour, and salt, and stir until completely incorporated.

Pour the batter into your partially baked pie crust, and bake until the filling has set and the crust is golden, 30 to 35 minutes. Let cool completely on a wire rack.

For the topping: In a bowl, beat the cream until stiff peaks form. Add the Caramel Sauce and beat until completely incorporated. Spread or pipe the caramel cream over the top of the pie, and drizzle the extra Caramel Sauce and fudge sauce over the top. Chill until ready to serve, or cut into wedges to serve immediately.

PECAN PIE

Pecan pie has recently become a favorite in my house, and it's, of course, a holiday classic. This version has a little slug of whiskey, which just adds to the depth of flavor. Plus, ya know, whiskey!

Preheat the oven to 350°F. In a large bowl, whisk together the eggs, dark corn syrup, brown sugar, melted butter, whiskey (if using), vanilla, cinnamon, and salt. Then stir in the flour.

Put the pecans into the prepared pie crust, and spread them evenly. Pour the egg mixture over the pecans.

Bake the pie until the filling is set—it should be just slightly jiggly in the middle—for 45 to 50 minutes. Serve warm or at room temperature, and cut into generous wedges.

MAKES 8 SERVINGS

3 eggs

1 cup dark corn syrup

½ cup firmly packed brown sugar

¼ cup unsalted butter, melted

2 tablespoons whiskey (optional)

1 teaspoon vanilla extract

¼ teaspoon ground cinnamon

¼ teaspoon salt

2 tablespoons all-purpose flour, sifted

2 cups roughly chopped pecans

1 Flaky Pie Crust (see page 202), unbaked

PEACH-BLUEBERRY PIE

Lattice pies are my favorite pies, mainly because they look so pretty. The method isn't very hard once you try it once either. This lattice is placed over a sweet blueberry-and-peach filling, and a touch of cinnamon and vanilla tie this pie up with a golden-brown bow.

MAKES 8 SERVINGS

2 cups blueberries

3 large ripe peaches, peeled, pitted, and diced

¾ cup sugar

¼ cup all-purpose flour

1½ teaspoons cornstarch

Finely grated zest and juice of 1 lemon

1 teaspoon vanilla extract

½ teaspoon ground cinnamon

1 Flaky Pie Crust (page 202), unbaked, plus the extra dough disk from the recipe

1 egg

2 tablespoons coarse sugar

Preheat the oven to 350°F. In a large bowl, stir together the blueberries, peaches, sugar, flour, cornstarch, lemon zest and juice, vanilla, and cinnamon. Pour this filling into your prepared pie pan with the bottom crust.

Unwrap the remaining dough disk and place it on a lightly floured work surface. Using a rolling pin, and working from the center outwards in all directions, roll the dough into a 10-inch round. Turn the dough and re-flour the surface and pin as needed to prevent sticking. Using a ruler and a paring knife, cut the dough into 1-inch strips.

To create the lattice top, place 5 to 6 dough strips next to one other on the pie, leaving a gap between the strips. Gently fold back every other strip on top of itself. Then place another strip at the halfway mark, perpendicular to the first strips. Return the folded over pieces to their original positions, and fold over the pieces that you skipped last time. Place another perpendicular strip. Fold the strips back down, and repeat across the pie. Cut off any excess on the edges of the pie, and pinch the edges together.

Beat the egg in a small bowl, and brush the lattice strips with the egg wash. Then sprinkle the coarse sugar over the top. Bake until the pie crust is golden brown and the filling is bubbling, 40 to 45 minutes. Let cool on a wire rack and cut into wedges to serve.

BACON, CHEDDAR & VEGGIE QUICHE

This savory, chile-spiked quiche is perfect for brunch. The great thing about quiche is that it's flexible. Throw in whatever vegetables you have, whatever cheese you prefer, and whatever meats you'd like. No matter what, it's going to turn out delicious.

Preheat the oven to 350°F. In a skillet, warm the olive oil over medium heat. Add the chopped onion and balsamic vinegar and cook, stirring, until reduced and caramelized, about 15 minutes. You want the onion to reach a deep caramelization. Add the garlic and continue cooking for a couple of minutes. Remove from the heat.

In a large bowl, beat together the eggs, milk, cream, salt, pepper, paprika, and chili powder. Then fold in the red pepper, jalapeño, bacon, and green onions. Set aside 1 handful of the cheddar cheese, then fold the rest into the egg mixture. Add the cooled onion and garlic mixture. Pour the egg mixture into a deep-dish pan lined with the pie crust dough, and sprinkle with the reserved cheese.

Carefully place the quiche in the oven, and bake until a cake tester inserted into the center comes out clean and the quiche is set, 45 to 60 minutes. Serve warm or at room temperature, and cut into wedges.

MAKES 6 TO 8 SERVINGS

1 teaspoon olive oil

½ yellow onion, chopped

1 teaspoon balsamic vinegar

3 cloves garlic, minced

8 eggs

¾ cup whole milk

¼ cup heavy cream

2 teaspoons salt

1 teaspoon freshly ground black pepper, plus more for sprinkling

½ teaspoon paprika

½ teaspoon chili powder

½ red bell pepper, chopped

1 jalapeño chile, seeds removed, chopped

6 to 7 pieces bacon, cooked and crumbled

2 green onions, chopped

1 cup shredded cheddar cheese

1 Flaky Pie Crust (see page 202), unbaked

TRIPLE-BERRY & APPLE GALETTES

A galette is just a fancy word for a flat pie. The combination of berries and apples isn't a very common one. But if you use a Granny Smith apple, the tart flavor is really nice next to sweet berries, all tucked into a pie crust.

MAKES 2 GALETTES, 16 SERVINGS

2 Granny Smith apples, peeled, cored, and chopped

1 pint blackberries

1 pint raspberries

1 pint strawberries, chopped

Juice of ½ lemon

1 tablespoon sugar

1 tablespoon cornstarch

2 Flaky Pie Crusts (see page 202), unbaked

1 egg, beaten

Vanilla ice cream for serving (optional)

Preheat the oven to 350°F and line 2 baking sheets with parchment paper or nonstick mats. In a large bowl, mix together the chopped apples, blackberries, raspberries, and chopped strawberries. Add the lemon juice, sugar, and cornstarch. Toss together.

Roll out the pie crust dough disks and carefully transfer 1 pie crust to a prepared baking sheet, and use a slotted spoon to place about half the fruit mixture in the center of the crust. Fold the edges of your crust over the berries, forming loose pleats all around the edges, leaving the center of the galette open. Repeat with the other crust and remaining filling on the other baking sheet. Brush each crust with the beaten egg.

Bake until the crust is browned on top and the filling is bubbling, 25 to 30 minutes. Serve warm, cut into wedges, with vanilla ice cream for an extra treat!

MINI APPLE GALETTES

Mini apple galettes are just the right size for one, and they're pretty stinkin' adorable to serve to a crowd. The trick here is to make sure you pinch the edges of the crust together pretty tightly, otherwise they fall apart in the oven. But trust me, they still taste incredible.

Preheat the oven to 375°F, and line 1 or 2 baking sheets with parchment paper or nonstick mats. In a large bowl, stir together the chopped apples, granulated sugar, brown sugar, softened butter, and cinnamon, until well mixed.

With the pie dough rolled out to about ¼ inch thick, use a 4-inch plain or fluted pastry cutter to cut out 8 to 10 rounds from the dough. Carefully transfer the dough rounds onto the prepared baking sheet(s). Spoon about 2 tablespoons of the apple filling onto each circle. Fold the edges of the circle up around the filling, forming loose pleats all around the edges, leaving the center of the galettes open. Pinch the dough together around the filling to hold it in. Brush the beaten egg over the outer crusts. Then sprinkle coarse sugar over the tops.

Bake until the crust is golden brown on the outer edges and the filling is bubbling, 20 to 25 minutes. Let cool on a wire rack before serving.

MAKES 8 TO 10 SERVINGS

4 Granny Smith apples, peeled, cored, and chopped

½ cup granulated sugar

½ cup firmly packed brown sugar

¼ cup unsalted butter, softened

2 teaspoons ground cinnamon

2 Flaky Pie Crusts (see page 202), unbaked

1 egg, beaten

2 to 3 tablespoons coarse sugar

BLACKBERRY MERINGUE TART

The key to making the perfect meringue pie is to make sure you don't overbeat the egg white mixture—it can be difficult to spread and form correctly if it's too stiff. Also, when using the broiler, keep your eyes on it! It browns really fast.

MAKES 8 SERVINGS

FOR THE CRUST

¾ cup unsalted butter, softened

½ cup powdered sugar

2 teaspoons vanilla extract

1½ cups all-purpose flour

¼ teaspoon salt

FOR THE BLACKBERRY CURD

4 cups blackberries (about 3 pints)

Finely grated zest of 1 lemon

Juice of 1 lemon plus enough
    water to equal ½ cup liquid

6 egg yolks

1 cup granulated sugar

⅛ teaspoon salt

1 teaspoon powdered unflavored
    gelatin

1 tablespoon cold water

Meringue (see page 207)

For the crust: Preheat the oven to 325°F, and lightly grease a 9-inch pie dish. In a bowl, beat together the butter and powdered sugar until fluffy. Add the vanilla and mix well. Add the flour and salt, and beat until combined. The mixture will be soft. Press the dough evenly into the greased dish. Poke a few holes in the bottom with a fork. Bake until the crust is golden brown, 25 to 30 minutes. The dough will puff a bit while baking.

For the blackberry curd: In a blender or food processor, blend the berries into a puree. Place a fine-mesh sieve over a saucepan and pour the puree through to remove the seeds. Add the lemon zest, juice and water mixture, egg yolks, sugar, and salt, and cook over medium-low heat, whisking often. Meanwhile, in a small bowl, pour the gelatin over the cold water, and let bloom. Then microwave on full power for 20 to 30 seconds to dissolve the gelatin. Whisk the gelatin into the berry mixture as it is cooking. Bring the mixture to a boil, and cook until thickened, 8 to 10 minutes. Pour the mixture through a clean strainer into a heatproof bowl. Spread the curd evenly in the prepared tart crust.

Turn on the broiler to low. Scoop the meringue onto the filling and spread all the way to the edges of the dish. Using a fork, fluff the meringue to give it a few peaks. Place the pie under the broiler until just dark golden, 5 to 10 minutes, but keep a close eye on it! Let the pie cool to room temperature on a wire rack, then chill completely in the refrigerator before serving.

ALMOND CREAM TART

This is my play off of a Bakewell tart, which is a traditional English dessert. It's almost like a soft cookie, and if you like the flavor of almond, you'll love this. You can swap out any jam you prefer here for the strawberry—raspberry or cherry would both be great choices.

In a large bowl, beat together the almond flour, granulated sugar, butter, and flour until blended. Add the whole egg, egg white, almond extract, and vanilla, and beat until smooth. Chill the mixture in the refrigerator for 30 minutes.

Preheat the oven to 350°F. Spread the strawberry jam in an even layer on the bottom of the partially baked tart crust. Then spread the almond flour mixture evenly over the top. Bake until the tart is golden brown on top, 30 to 35 minutes. Let cool completely in the pan on a wire rack. Dust with powdered sugar, if desired, before slicing into wedges and serving.

MAKES 8 TO 10 SERVINGS

1 cup almond flour

¾ cup granulated sugar

½ cup unsalted butter, softened

2 tablespoons all-purpose flour

1 egg

1 egg white

½ teaspoon almond extract

½ teaspoon vanilla extract

½ cup strawberry jam (or jam of your choice)

1 Tart Crust (see page 203), partially baked

Powdered sugar for dusting (optional)

CANDY BAR TART

We all like candy bars—don't lie to me, I know you've got a favorite. This tart happens to resemble my husband's favorite bar, with a couple of twists. Layers of sweet tart dough, caramel-coated pecans, and dense chocolate ganache make this bad boy something you'll be craving too!

MAKES 8 TO 10 SERVINGS

FOR THE CARAMEL LAYER

2 cups sugar

¾ cup heavy cream

½ cup unsalted butter, softened

1 teaspoon vanilla extract

¼ teaspoon table salt

1 cup chopped pecans

1 Tart Crust (see page 203),
  fully baked

FOR THE CHOCOLATE LAYER

⅔ cup heavy cream

1 cup dark chocolate chips

1½ teaspoons coarse salt (optional)

For the caramel layer: In a saucepan, cook the sugar over medium-high heat until it has liquefied and become a dark amber color, about 10 minutes. While the sugar is cooking, stir it occasionally. If you've reached a dark amber color but still have some chunks of sugar, fish them out with a spoon and discard. Remove from the heat, and add the heavy cream while whisking continuously. The mixture will be very hot and will bubble up, so it's best to use a long-handled whisk. Whisk until the mixture is completely smooth, and then whisk in the butter. Stir in the vanilla and table salt. If you have some lumps in your caramel, place it back on the heat for a few minutes, whisking constantly. Place a wire mesh strainer over a heatproof bowl and pour through the caramel to remove any remaining small lumps. Let cool for about 20 minutes. Stir in the chopped pecans.

Pour the caramel mixture into the cooled tart crust, and spread evenly. Chill in the refrigerator for 30 minutes.

For the chocolate layer: In a heatproof bowl, microwave the cream until boiling. Add the chocolate chips, and whisk until the mixture is smooth, shiny, and thick. Pour over the chilled caramel layer, and spread evenly. Evenly sprinkle the coarse salt over the top, if using. Cover and chill the tart for several hours. Cut into wedges and serve cold.

BOURBON-SPIKED CHOCOLATE-CARAMEL TART

This tart is made up of sweet, dense chocolate cream, and drizzled with a bourbon caramel sauce. That's right, I said bourbon, and I meant it.

For the filling: Place the chocolate in a large heatproof bowl, and place a wire mesh strainer on top. In a small bowl, whisk the egg yolks and sugar until thick and pale. In a saucepan, stir together the milk, vanilla, and salt, and bring to a low boil. While whisking constantly, slowly pour about half of the hot liquid into the yolk mixture to temper the yolks, and then pour back into the saucepan. Whisk in the cornstarch and cook until the mixture has started to thicken, 1 to 2 minutes. Pour the hot mixture through the mesh strainer over the chocolate. Whisk the mixture until the chocolate has melted completely and the filling is smooth and uniform. Pour the filling over the crust and spread evenly. Cover with plastic wrap. Chill in the refrigerator for at least 2 hours.

For the Caramel Sauce: In a saucepan, stir together the sugar and water. Without stirring, bring the mixture to a boil and continue boiling until it has reached a dark amber color, 10 to 15 minutes. Seriously, do not stir it even once while it's boiling. Remove from the heat and add the heavy cream. The mixture will bubble and may feel slightly hard before it softens, but just continue to whisk and it will smooth out. Add the butter, bourbon, vanilla, and salt and stir until combined. Cool the sauce slightly before serving. (If you're not using it right away, you can store the sauce in a mason jar in the fridge and re-heat in the microwave.) Drizzle about half the caramel sauce (or as much as you prefer) over the tart before cutting into wedges to serve.

MAKES 10 TO 12 SERVINGS

FOR THE FILLING

8 ounces dark chocolate, chopped

4 egg yolks

3 tablespoons sugar

1⅔ cups whole milk

1 teaspoon vanilla extract

¼ teaspoon salt

1 tablespoon cornstarch

1 Tart Crust (see page 203), fully baked

FOR THE CARAMEL SAUCE

1 cup sugar

¼ cup water

½ cup heavy cream

1 tablespoon butter

1 tablespoon bourbon

1 teaspoon vanilla extract

½ teaspoon salt

TOMATO-GOAT CHEESE TART

This tart screams summertime. The combination of tomatoes, goat cheese, and honey is everything, and it's a great choice for a meatless Monday dinner, if you're into that kind of thing. Or just lunchtime, if you're into that kind of thing.

MAKES 8 TO 10 SERVINGS

FOR THE CRUST

1½ cups shredded cheddar cheese
(from a block, not pre-shredded)

¾ cup all-purpose flour

¼ cup unsalted butter, softened

1 to 2 tablespoons whole milk

FOR THE FILLING

3 tablespoons unsalted butter

1 large yellow onion,
cut into half-moons

2 teaspoons sugar

1 teaspoon freshly ground
black pepper

1 teaspoon salt

¾ cup crumbled goat cheese

⅓ cup Greek yogurt

2 egg whites

2 to 3 large heirloom tomatoes,
cut into ¼-inch slices

4 to 5 mini heirloom tomatoes,
halved (optional)

1 to 2 tablespoons honey

For the crust: Preheat the oven to 350°F. Lightly grease a 10-inch tart pan with a removable bottom. In a food processor, pulse the cheddar cheese, flour, and softened butter until just combined. Add 1 tablespoon of the milk and pulse until the mixture starts to come together like a dough. If it does not come together, add the second tablespoon of milk. Roll out the dough on a floured work surface to fit into your tart pan, and transfer it to the pan, pressing it into the corners. Trim the edges. Bake until the crust is just starting to set and brown, 8 to 10 minutes. Set aside. Leave the oven set at 350°F.

For the filling: In a large skillet over medium heat, melt the butter. Add the onion, sugar, pepper, and ½ teaspoon of the salt. Cook, stirring regularly, until the onion reaches a dark golden, caramelized color, 20 to 25 minutes. Set aside. In a bowl, beat together the goat cheese, yogurt, egg whites, and the remaining ½ teaspoon salt. Spread the goat cheese mixture evenly into the prepared tart crust. Arrange the caramelized onions and tomatoes on top. Bake until the edges of the crust are golden and the top of the pie is just browning, 30 to 35 minutes. Then turn the oven to a low broil and cook until the tomatoes just start to brown, 1 to 2 minutes. Remove the tart from the oven, and drizzle honey on top to taste. Cut into wedges and enjoy warm.

CLASSIC BERRY COBBLER

This classic biscuit-topped cobbler is simple and quick to throw together, and who doesn't like dessert in a hurry? The indulgent ice cream is easy too, can be made ahead, and doesn't require an ice cream maker.

Preheat the oven to 425°F and lightly grease an 11-by-17-inch rectangular or 8-inch square baking dish.

For the fruit filling: In a saucepan, combine the raspberries, blackberries, blueberries, granulated sugar, lemon juice, and cornstarch. Stir everything together, and cook over medium-high heat until boiling. The mixture will begin to thicken. Pour into the prepared dish.

For the biscuit topping: In a bowl, stir together the flour, oats, granulated sugar, baking powder, and salt. Cut in the butter with a pastry blender or your fingertips until the mixture is crumbly. Pour in the buttermilk and vanilla, and stir together until the mixture has formed into larger, soft crumbs, and has become a bit sticky. Do not overwork the mixture. Place chunks of the topping all over the top of the berry mixture, spacing it evenly. Sprinkle the top with the coarse sugar. Bake until the top is golden brown, 16 to 18 minutes. Enjoy warm, spooned into bowls with a scoop of Whiskey Vanilla Ice Cream.

For the Whiskey Vanilla Ice Cream: (Adults only on this one, guys—the whiskey is not cooked out, and the flavor is strong.) In a large bowl, whip the cream until very stiff peaks form. Beat in the sweetened condensed milk, bourbon, and vanilla. Transfer to freezer-safe containers, and freeze for at least 2 hours.

MAKES 6 TO 8 SERVINGS

FOR THE FRUIT FILLING

2 pints raspberries

2 pints blackberries

1 pint blueberries

¼ cup granulated sugar

Juice of ½ lemon

1 tablespoon cornstarch

FOR THE BISCUIT TOPPING

1 cup all-purpose flour

2 tablespoons old-fashioned rolled oats

1½ tablespoons granulated sugar

1½ teaspoons baking powder

¼ teaspoon salt

¼ cup unsalted butter, chilled and cubed

½ cup chilled buttermilk

1 teaspoon vanilla extract

1 tablespoon coarse sugar

FOR THE WHISKEY VANILLA ICE CREAM

2½ cups heavy cream

1 can (14 ounces) sweetened condensed milk

3 tablespoons bourbon whiskey

2 teaspoons vanilla extract

INDEX

ABOUT THE AUTHOR

Nicole Hampton is the writer behind the blog Dougheyed.com, where she shares recipes sweet and savory alike. Dough-eyed has been featured in several local publications. She's been baking since childhood, and pulls so much inspiration from her grandmothers and mother.

By day, Nicole works in SEO and social media marketing for an agency in Denver. When she's not baking, you can find her hanging out with her wild dog, Sage, listening to podcasts, or eating breakfast for every single meal of the day.

ACKNOWLEDGMENTS

Thanks go to my family: Mom, Dad, and Jesse, who always have excitement and love to share with me, and who have always appreciated my cooking and baking, even when it was bad. (Sorry I made you hate cinnamon things, Jesse!)

To my extended family and best friends: the Crawfords, McKinnons, Hamptons, and Orrs. Thank you for always joining us for food and games and laughs, and for being there for all the ups and downs for so long. And thanks, Matt—you always make me feel great about my cooking on football Sundays.

To all my GDWer's: You've been the best taste-testers! Thank you for celebrating all the small and the big wins with me every day, and for generally putting up with me—I know I can be annoying, even though I bring you guys a lot of cake. Special GDW thanks to Analiese and Meg, who helped me figure out this contract nonsense!

To Jen, and everyone at Graphic Arts Books, who made this far-off goal become a reality for me.

Last, to my favorite man in the world, my husband, Jacob. Thank you for listening to all my late-night and early-morning and mid-day ramblings about this book, and for taming all my nerves over it, and for countless dishes washed, and for going to the grocery store for forgotten ingredients, like, all the time. Thank you for giving me honest opinions, even though I didn't always want them. Thank you for always going to buy me a slice of pie on days when I didn't feel like baking.

Library of Congress Cataloging-in-Publication Data

Names: Hampton, Nicole, author.
Title: Sugar high : sweet and savory baking in your high-altitude
    kitchen / by Nicole Hampton.
Description: Berkeley : Graphic Arts Books, [2018] | Includes index. |
    Identifiers: LCCN 2018002539 (print) | LCCN 2018017299 (ebook) |
    ISBN 9781513261263 (ebook) | ISBN 9781513261249 (pbk.) |
    ISBN 9781513261256 (hardcover)
Subjects: LCSH: Desserts. | High altitude cooking. | LCGFT: Cookbooks.
Classification: LCC TX773 (ebook) | LCC TX773 .H249 2018 (print) |
    DDC 641.86--dc23
LC record available at https://lccn.loc.gov/2018002539

Printed in China
21 20 19 18 1 2 3 4 5

Edited by Kristen Tate and Becky Duffet
Indexed by Elizabeth Parsons
Image credit: pages 6-7: Aon_Anda/Shutterstock.com;
pages 8, 13, and 232: Courtney Jewell Photography

WestWinds Press®
An imprint of

GRAPHIC ARTS
BOOKS®

GraphicArtsBooks.com

Proudly distributed by Ingram Publisher Services

GRAPHIC ARTS BOOKS
Publishing Director: Jennifer Newens
Marketing Manager: Angela Zbornik
Editor: Olivia Ngai
Design & Production: Rachel Lopez Metzger